My Hobby is Bird Watching

My Hobby is

BIRD WATCHING

MARY P. PETTIT

Hart Book Company   •   New York

Manufactured in the United States of America

Design by Stefan Salter

Contents

Illustration Credits

Least sandpipers on shore

Scissor-tailed flycatcher

Chapter One

BIRD WATCHING IS FUN

If you are looking for a hobby that is filled with fun and adventure, try bird watching. Bird watching is a hobby you can follow any time of year, anywhere you happen to be. But like any other hobby, the more you go into it and the more skilled you become, the more fun it is and the more thrills you find.

BIRD WATCHING ALL OVER THE WORLD

Perhaps when you first think about bird watching, it seems rather dull. But do not be fooled by the magazine or newspaper cartoons showing a group of elderly ladies looking up in a tree in the city park. Bird watching means much more than that to many people, and some of the best bird watchers in the country are former athletes who are also some of the most rugged outdoors men you ever saw. Bird watching is possible in a city park or even in your back yard. But it also leads people to the tops of mountains, to Arctic tundra, to tropical jungles, to desert wastes, and to the middle of vast oceans.

More serious bird watchers must also be skilled mountain climbers, expert canoeists, experienced campers and hikers who can spend a day walking for miles without tiring.

In bird watching you will find the same adventure that takes big-game hunters to deepest Africa or big-game fishermen to the waters of the South Seas.

Bird watchers hunt with binoculars, telescope, or camera, rather than with gun or fishing rod. But the thrill of seeing an unusual bird or capturing its image on film is as great as bringing home a trophy head or a record-breaking fish.

Look at the pictures in a good bird guide. Look at pictures, for example, of the water ouzel, the rosy finch, the trumpeter swan, the gannet, the water turkey, the roseate spoonbill, the scissor-tailed flycatcher, the wood ibis, the greater shearwater, the puffin, the albatross, or the tiny black rail.

To see these birds in one year, or even two—unless you were extremely lucky—you would have to travel some twenty thousand miles perhaps, from the Gaspé Peninsula in easternmost Quebec to Florida, then to the Pacific Coast. You would visit marshes and swamps such as the Everglades, travel hundreds of miles offshore by boat, climb mountains ten thousand or more feet high, climb down rocky canyons, and drive or walk through the desert or along Wyoming lakes. You would see some of the largest and most spectacular of North American birds, and there is adventure involved in finding each one of them.

Pair of adult trumpeter swans

BIRD WATCHING CLOSE TO HOME

But closer to home, you can find similar adventures in any swamp, marsh, pond, forest, or field. If you've never seen an oriole build its nest on the very tip of a high branch in an elm; or found the tiny postage-stamp-sized nest of the hummingbird; or watched a killdeer try to lure you away from its nest by pretending it has a broken wing—you can find bird watching adventures almost in your back yard.

If you have never had a blue jay dive at your head trying to chase you away, or if you've never had wild birds feed from your hand; if you have never thrilled to the beauty of a wood duck swimming through the reeds, or to the whistle of the air through the wings of geese as they soar in to land; if you have never been covered with goose flesh when a screech owl cries weirdly from a tree when you least expect it, or if you have never been startled half out of your shoes by a grouse roaring up from between your feet—you have thrills ahead that you never dreamed of as you look for birds.

You can have fun watching birds such as these quite close to home. None are rare or hard to find.

BIRD WATCHING AND YOUR OTHER INTERESTS

Whatever your interests, you can tie them to bird watching, and, in addition, get the benefits of a healthy outdoor hobby.

Suppose your interest is music, either playing or listening to the classics. Have you ever heard a wood thrush sing its song at twilight, or even a robin? Have you heard a winter wren sing its song beside a roaring mountain stream? Has any composer ever duplicated this music for flute or violin?

Have you heard the cry of the wild goose flock as it flies over in the fall or the call of the loon echoing among the hills that surround the northern lake? Have you heard the call of the whippoorwill in the spring, or the song of the tanager from among the apple blossoms in the orchard?

To the bird watcher these are comparable to any music created

MY HOBBY IS
BIRD WATCHING

12

Great blue heron,
Clear Lake
National Wildlife
Refuge, California

Killdeer on nest in gravel pit

Gull (California)

by man.

If your interest is art, studying the color and technique of famous painters, watch birds in their native habitat for similar beauty. Look at a cardinal in a flowering dogwood; an oriole in a pear tree in blossom; look at an egret in a mangrove or a heron feeding on the shore among many colored shells.

You will find color beyond description as you watch wild birds in action.

Perhaps you have scientific ambitions and want to become a research scientist by profession. Or perhaps you would like to try it out first to see how you like it. Ornithology—the scientific end of bird watching—is a relatively new science and there is still much to be learned about birds and why they act as they do.

MORE INFORMATION NEEDED ABOUT BIRDS

Some basic information about some rather common birds is not known by scientists. How long it takes some birds' eggs to hatch; how some birds build their nests; which parent hatches the eggs; where other birds nest—all are examples of things professional ornithologists are trying to find.

Experiments are still being carried out to find out why birds migrate, what some birds eat, or where they spend the winter.

Interestingly, too, the habits of some birds change over the years as they become adapted to man's changes of the landscape.

For example, barn owls have not always nested in barns because before man settled this country there were no barns. Obviously, too, chimney swifts did not previously nest in chimneys. Barn owls don't all nest in barns now, nor do swifts in chimneys—but they are examples of birds that have changed their habits. Other birds are changing a little at a time, all the time. Perhaps you can observe these changes and contribute to the scientists' knowledge.

HOW BIRD WATCHING CAN BRING NEW FRIENDS

Bird watching may be filled with adventure, depending upon how seriously you take it. One of the interesting things you will find will be the other people you meet who are interested in birds.

There is a bird club downtown in New York City, centering on famous Wall Street. Several times a month, its members spend their lunch hour on the waterfront or in city parks looking for birds. They see some seventy-five species a year in a place where it is hard to believe they would see any. Some are quite unusual.

One day one of the members walked by City Hall and noticed several windows crowded with people. They all seemed to be looking up in a tree. He looked, too, and saw a barred owl. That night the newspapers carried the story. The City Council took a recess so that all might see the unusual bird—unusual, that is, when seen on a busy city street.

Members of that bird club include stockbrokers, lawyers, office clerks, newspapermen, merchants, and business executives. They all have a common hobby.

Blue jay

Another bird club has among its members a city fireman, a tugboat captain, a newsreel photographer, a radio announcer, a newspaper columnist, a writer, advertising executives, schoolteachers, and professional scientists. These people gather together regularly to talk about birds and exchange experiences.

At least one president of the United States has claimed bird watching as a hobby, as do several Hollywood actors, one movie director, two state governors, one TV notable, one famous criminal, and a host of other well-known people.

When you start out on a bird watching expedition, you can never tell whom you will meet. But whoever it is, you can be sure he will be interesting to talk to.

DISCOVERIES THROUGH BIRD WATCHING

Another interesting outcome of knowing birds is being able to explain newspaper stories that crop up at regular intervals.

Each spring, if you read the papers frequently enough, you will read about "crazy" robins. The story will tell in detail about robins that fly at windows or the shiny hubcaps on cars, pecking at the window or hubcap till it seems that they will kill themselves. The writer takes great joy in describing the crazy robins. But the birds aren't crazy, as you know if you are a bird watcher. You will know that the robins are only trying to chase away what they think is another robin.

Several years ago another story was printed in many papers about "ghosts" in a small town in upstate New York, and occasional variations appear during or after hunting seasons each fall.

In each case the story has to do with ladies who wear small fur hats or hunters who wear fur caps or hats. The ladies were walking down the street at night when suddenly something hit them on the head and their hats were gone. In the case of the hunters, they went out one night to get wood for the stove, or a bucket of water from the spring. Halfway to the woodpile, the "ghost" got their hats.

In both cases the hats were found the next day a hundred feet or so from where the "ghost" struck. But the stories go to some length describing the "ghosts" that steal hats.

The truth of these stories is that owls took the hats, thinking they were small animals upon which they feed. When they found that the hats were really only fur, they dropped them and flew away.

If you know that owls fly silently and make no sound whatever, it is easy to understand how the ghost stories got started.

Other stories will describe "mixed up" birds—geese that fly north when they should fly south, or starlings that fly west when they should fly south. Recently some New Jersey papers have described "mixed up" blackbirds that were flying south in the spring.

In truth these birds were not mixed up. They were not migrating in the sense of flying south in fall or north in spring. The birds were flying back to a roost at night—probably some protected place where they were sheltered from wind and cold after feeding all day. When you become experienced as a bird watcher, you can answer many of the questions like these that are written up in newspapers around the country.

The chapters that follow in this book will tell you how to get started as a bird watcher—how to learn birds, how to have fun watching them, how to attract them to your yard or park, and where to go to see some of the more interesting birds of this country.

If you take up birds as a hobby, you will have few dull moments for the rest of your life. For whenever time hangs heavy on, your hands, you can watch for birds. There's always something new and interesting to look for.

*American egret
in nesting colony*

Chapter Two

WHAT BIRD IS THAT?

Learning birds, knowing them so you can call them by name, is not as difficult as you may think. But go about it with a method and try to learn a few at a time rather than many at once. The best way to learn birds is to go out and look at them, one at a time, and learn one at a time.

You probably know some birds right now. Robins, for example, English sparrows, and starlings are quite common in most places. Nearly everyone has seen downy woodpeckers, too—those little woodpeckers with the red spot on the back of the head that run up and down tree trunks probing the bark for insects. Blue jays and house wrens, crows and blackbirds, are other common birds that you have probably seen out in the country. You probably have seen gulls and ducks along the water. If so, you have a good start right now.

BIRDS YOU CAN SEE IN THE WINTER

Strange as it may seem, late fall, winter, and early spring are good times to start learning to recognize birds. These are good times because there probably are not so many birds to be seen as in late spring or summer and you can learn birds one or two at a time.

Western grebe

In late fall, winter, and early spring, you will see, in general, two groups of birds—those that live in your neighborhood all year round and those that live there just in the winter. During this season, the trees have lost their leaves and it is easier to see the birds.

If you live near water, you will probably be able to see ducks and other water birds that are rather easy to identify.

Depending upon where you live, the year-round residents may be birds that even nest right in your yard or in a neighboring park. Blue jays, downy woodpeckers, song sparrows, crows, killdeer, cardinals, starlings, and cowbirds are examples of birds that are found all year round in many localities.

But during the winter, birds that spend the summer far to the north may migrate to your area for the winter. Some of the birds listed above may be in that class, and in addition you might see gulls, geese, grebes, and several kinds of ducks if you live near lakes, ponds, or rivers; or you might see such birds as juncos, pine siskins, grosbeaks, crossbills, or some owls.

These birds may live in your area all winter, then fly back north again in the spring to nest and raise their young.

BIRDS YOU CAN SEE IN THE SPRING

As spring comes on, more birds seem to arrive every day, until every bush or tree seems alive with bird activity. Again you will find that these birds fall into two general categories. First will be those birds that will stay and nest in your neighborhood. Birds such as the robin, oriole, tanager, meadow lark, flicker, redwing, and others, spend the winter in the south and fly north in the spring to nest.

In the second group will be birds that have spent the winter in the south, but nest far to the north. Many of the shore birds—birds like sandpipers and plovers—are in this group.

Other birds might be the warblers, thrushes, and some of the sparrows. The sandpipers and plovers, for example, may nest within the Arctic Circle—but they visit your area briefly during their migration flight.

LEARNING WHERE BIRDS LIVE

As you learn the names of the birds you see, try to place them in the proper group: year-round resident, winter resident, spring migrant, or summer resident. You can do this by reading some of the books listed at the end of this book. When you see a new bird and look up its picture and description, find out all you can about the bird—where it spends the winter, where it nests, the kind of place you might expect to find it, and the kind of place in which it builds its nest. Do not be satisfied with learning just the name. Frequently the thing that makes bird watching thrilling and interesting is the bird itself.

For example, a few years ago my family and I spent the summer in the western part of the United States. One of the birds that we saw frequently was the western tanager, a beautiful yellow-and-black colored bird with a red head, a little smaller than a robin. According to the bird books, the western tanager is found in the mountains and foothills of all the western states and spends the winter south of the United States. Yet one cold February day on the beach of Long Island, New York, we saw a western tanager. We had made a rather spectacular find because the western tanager wasn't supposed to be there. But if we hadn't known that, the thrill of seeing the bird would have been lost.

In the same way, we once found a red-bellied woodpecker on Long Island. This woodpecker is essentially a southern bird, and to see one in winter so far north was most unusual. If we had not known that the bird was out of place on Long Island in January, it would have been just another bird.

Knowing where birds are supposed to be at any time of year by reading, helps you identify the birds you see. If you see something unusual, check three or four times to be sure. You may even ask another bird watcher to check your find. Birds can be confusing sometimes, and it's always well to be sure.

Woodpecker:

Beak

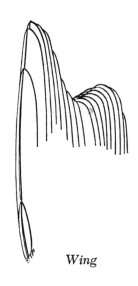

Wing

LEARNING THE TERRAIN BIRDS PREFER

Another hint that will make bird identification easier is to know the

Tail

Foot

kind of natural area that birds prefer—that is, marsh, pond, woods, field, or beach. Just as some people prefer to live in a city or must live there because they work in the city, and other people live in the country or must live there, birds, too, have rather definite places where they prefer to live. Some birds are named after the place where you generally see them.

Woodpeckers, for example, are most often found in the woods, or at least on trees, where they feed on insects found in the bark. Marsh hawks are so named because they generally are seen over marshes. Meadow larks are usually found in fields or meadows, as are field sparrows. Sandpipers and plovers are called shore birds because they feed along the shores of bays, rivers, ponds, or oceans. The names barn owl and chimney swift tell you immediately where you might expect to find them, as do the names barn swallow, cliff swallow, and spruce grouse.

You would expect to find ducks on or near water, and the name kingfisher tells you that the bird eats fish.

LEARNING WHAT BIRDS EAT

As you see birds, remember where you saw them, the kind of natural area in which they were found. Then read about them and find out what they eat. That, too, will give you a clue as to where to find them.

If you read that a bird eats weed seeds—goldfinches and sparrows , for example, do—you will look for them along roadsides, in fields, or along fence rows. If you know that an osprey is called a fish hawk, you will look near water. Birds that eat insects frequently are found in trees or flying over fields where they catch insects on the wing.

Knowing where birds prefer to live and what they eat can be of tremendous help in finding them and identifying them.

USING BIRD GUIDES

To identify birds in the easiest way, unless you can go out bird watching with an expert, you will need a good bird guide. In the East, two

Hawk:

Head

Beak

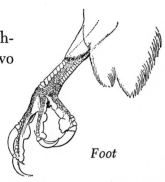

Foot

good ones are available:

Field Guide to the Birds, by Roger Tory Peterson. Boston, Houghton Mifflin Company, $3.75.

Audubon Bird Guide, by Richard Pough. Garden City, N. Y., Doubleday & Company, $3.50.

Read carefully the introductions to these books for further hints on identification.

GENERAL CLASSIFICATION OF BIRDS

Even with a good illustrated bird guide you can still be confused unless you know something about the birds you are likely to see. First, you should be able to place any bird you see in a general group or family. Then, using the guide and pictures, you can find the exact species.

Generally, the common birds you will see may be placed in one of the following groups:

WADING BIRDS   Herons, egrets, and bitterns are in this group of birds which have long legs, long necks, and long, pointed bills. You usually see them wading in shallow water looking for small fish.

WATERFOWL   Ducks and geese are in this group and are usually seen on or near water or marshes. Ducks are divided into two groups: Those that feed by tipping up and dabbling in shallow water and those that dive for food.

Young little blue herons

Jack snipe

Young bald eagle

BIRDS OF PREY Hawks, vultures, and eagles are in this group of generally large birds. They have hooked beaks and strong feet and feed on small animals such as mice and rats, amphibians, snakes, fish, and other birds. You usually see them soaring overhead or perched on a dead snag, from which they watch for prey.

GROUSE AND QUAIL These are birds that somewhat resemble chickens. Some are found in brushy areas, others in fields or prairies. Prairie chicken, ruffed grouse, spruce grouse, and sage hens are in this group. Quail are smaller than grouse and are easily distinguished from them. These birds are usually seen on the ground.

SHORE BIRDS This is a group of small wading birds found along streams, ponds, or the seashore. Some kinds live in fields and prairies. They have long probing bills and probe for small water animals or grubs in the soil. Sandpipers, killdeer, snipe, and woodcock are in this group.

GULLS AND TERNS These are long-winged, strong, flying birds found near large bodies of salt or fresh water. Gulls usually feed on the surface, while terns dive for their food. Herring, ring-billed, western, and California gulls and black, common and least terns are probably most often seen.

WOODPECKERS Flickers, red headed, downy and red-bellied wood-peckers, and sapsuckers are probably the commonest birds in this group. They are usually seen climbing tree trunks, probing the bark for insects. In flight, they flap several times, then pause, giving them an up-and-down sort of flight.

FLYCATCHERS These birds generally perch on bare twigs or power lines, every once in a while flying off to catch an insect. In between times they sit quite still, occasionally jerking their tails. Kingbirds, phoebes, and flycatchers are the common birds of this group.

SWALLOWS These are smallish birds with long, slender wings seen most often as they fly gracefully about over field or water chasing insects. Tree swallows, barn swallows, and martins are members of this group.

JAYS In general, jays are birds of the woodlands, where their large size, long tails, and bluish or gray color help identify them. Blue jays and Florida jays are found in the East, and the magpies, California jays, and Steller's jays, in the West.

THRASHERS This is a group of robin-sized birds with slender bills, generally curving downward. They are seen on the ground or in low shrubs. Mockingbirds, catbirds, and thrashers are in this group.

THRUSHES This group includes the robin, bluebird, and thrushes. With the exception of the bluebird, all are generally brownish on the back with speckled breasts. They are all known for their beautiful songs, and are usually seen feeding on or near the ground.

WARBLERS These are small, brightly colored insect-eating birds with fine bills and flitting habits. They are birds of the woodlands, usually seen at the tops of trees or at the tips of the branches of shrubs. Some of them are: myrtle warbler, Audubon's warbler, yellow warbler, black-and-white warbler.

Great crested flycatcher at nest

*Western meadow lark
hiding in grass*

MEADOW LARKS, BLACKBIRDS, AND ORIOLES These birds are found in several wildlife communities: bobolinks, meadow larks, and cowbirds in fields; orioles in high trees; grackles in marshes or woods; and redwings in marshes. Most of them are brightly colored and all have distinctive songs.

FINCHES AND SPARROWS Birds in this group all have strong, cone-shaped bills adapted for crushing or cracking seeds. They are found in almost all wildlife communities. Cardinals, grosbeaks, sparrows, towhees, and juncos are all in this group.

Black-billed magpie in act of pilfering a hen's egg from a dummy nest

IDENTIFYING BIRDS BY FAMILY

When you know birds at least by family, you can identify them by the process of elimination. You know immediately what the bird isn't, and you can narrow it down finally to what it is. You can do it rather quickly, too, if you know where the bird should be and, generally, what it should be doing. These things usually are more helpful than trying to figure out a bird's size.

For example, you frequently read about birds being larger or smaller than a robin or smaller than a crow. That's helpful information if there is a crow or a robin standing nearby for comparison. But it doesn't happen just that way, and many times exact size is difficult to judge. Light plays tricks on you, and birds may look larger or smaller than they really are. Or they may be moving swiftly or may be in an unusual position, so that their size is difficult to judge.

Generally, identification is easier if you read a little about birds ahead of time and know where they are likely to be seen, what they are likely to be eating, or what they may be doing.

IDENTIFYING BIRDS BY SONG AND CALL

In addition to sight observations, there are two other ways to identify birds, and both provide as positive identification as if you actually held the bird in your hand.

First is the bird song, call, or alarm note. With practice you will soon be able to identify many common birds by the song or call.

Record album: "Songbirds of America"

You've probably already heard robins, song sparrows, crows, jays, and ducks and know how different and distinct their songs or calls are. Some birds are named after their song or call—or rather their name is a verbal description of their song or call. The whippoorwill, poorwill, chuck-will's-widow, bobwhite, chickadee, and towhee are examples. By the very name "catbird" you may reasonably expect the call to sound something like a cat's meeow.

All birds have distinctive songs and calls. At first you may be confused and think they sound alike, and sometimes the songs of the birds in one family do sound much alike to the newcomer. But as you learn more about birds, you will be able to tell them apart by their calls, just as you can tell people by their voices.

There are several good phonograph records that will help you learn calls and songs.

RECORDS PUBLISHED BY CORNELL UNIVERSITY, ITHACA, N. Y.:

    Music and Bird Songs 10-inch LP record. $5.00.

    The Mockingbird Sings 10-inch 78-record. $2.50.

    Western Bird Songs 10-inch 78-record. $2.50.

    Florida Bird Songs 10-inch 78-record. $2.50.

    American Bird Songs Vol. I, 72 songs in six 10-inch 78-records. $7.75.

    American Bird Songs Vol. II, 51 songs on one 12-inch LP record. $7.75.

RECORDS PUBLISHED BY BOOK RECORDS, NEW YORK, N. Y.:

    Songbirds of America. One 10-inch LP record with accompanying text and illustrations of common back yard birds. $4.95.

Song sparrow— young just after leaving nest

IDENTIFYING BIRDS BY THE SIGNS THEY LEAVE

Another way to identify birds, besides by sight and sound, is by tracks or other signs. To identify birds in this way takes much more practice, and to be good at it, you will have to become an outdoors detective, to have a keen sense of observation and to find tiny details that the average person does not see.

Frequently along the edges of ponds or streams, along the beach or on mud flats, or even around mud puddles on dirt roads you can find bird tracks in the soft earth or mud. These tracks are just as positive identification to the skilled bird watcher as seeing the bird itself.

Old nests are an excellent means of identification, too. Birds all make their nests in different ways, and, with practice, you can tell a bird by its nest very easily. The hanging nest of the oriole, the more or less crude platform of the mourning dove, the hole in the tree of the downy woodpecker or flicker, all are very distinctive, and when you see them, you know those birds nest in your area.

But other signs may be found, too. Feathers, for example, are frequently found. When you know birds, you can identify these feathers. Owl pellets—the thumb-sized bundles of fur and bones of mice that owls spit out because they cannot digest them—are frequently found under pine or spruce trees. The size and shape of the pellet tells you the kind of owl that was there, and by picking apart the pellet, you can often find skulls that help you identify small mammals of the area.

If you walk along dirt roads in the woods, you will sometimes find shallow holes in the dust—unmistakable signs that grouse or pheasants have been dusting themselves to help remove insects or lice that infest them.

Sometimes you may even find dead birds or the remains of birds, and be able to identify them by the feathers, bones, or skulls.

Seeing live birds is the most fun. Sight observations should be practiced first. But there are other ways to identify birds, and you should not neglect them either. The three ways together are sometimes needed for definite identification of unusual species.

Grouse:

Beak

Wing

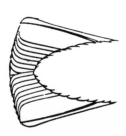

Tail

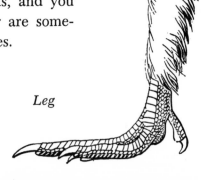

Leg

Chapter Three

BIRD WATCHING EQUIPMENT

Like any other hobby or sport, successful bird watching requires certain equipment. Unlike many other hobbies, the equipment need not be expensive or elaborate.

BINOCULARS

Undoubtedly the most basic equipment for bird watching is a good pair of binoculars—the best you can afford to buy. Field glasses are good as a starter, until you are sure that you like bird watching as a long-time hobby. But field glasses have their disadvantages, discussed on p. 32, and any serious bird watcher will soon realize that binoculars are a necessity. Fortunately, adequate binoculars now cost little more than field glasses did ten years ago.

The most desirable thing to look for in selecting binoculars for bird watching is light-gathering ability. This is the factor in binoculars that enables you to see color and to distinguish markings in poor light. Enough time is spent looking at birds in the poor light of early morning or late afternoon, or even in dark woods, so that your ability to see color and obscure markings is important.

You may have seen advertisements for binoculars or may have seen binoculars in stores. You may know that binoculars are frequently called by their formula of construction, such as 6 x 24; 6 x 30: 7 x 35; 7 x 50; 8 x 40, etc.

Light binoculars

MAGNIFICATION

The first number in the formula—the smaller number—refers to the power of magnification. If you use a 6-power binocular, a bird thirty feet away looks roughly the same as it would look five feet away without binoculars. If you had a 7-power binocular and looked at a bird twenty-eight feet away, it would be the same as seeing it at four feet without binoculars. In other words, the power is the number of times the lenses magnify the image you see.

The second number—24, 30, 35, or 50—refers to the diameter of the front lens of the binocular in millimeters. A 6 x 30 binocular is 6-power with a 30 millimeter diameter front (or objective) lens.

LIGHT-GATHERING POWER

To figure the relative light-gathering power, you divide the diameter of the front lens by the power, and square the number you get. Here is the way you would find the light-gathering power of a 6 x 30 binocular: $30 \div 6 = 5$ and $5 \times 5 = 25$. The light-gathering power of the 6 x 30 binocular is 25.

Within certain limits, the higher the light-gathering power of the binocular, the better it is for bird watching. In the opinion of many bird watchers, the best binocular is a 7 x 35. This glass has a light-gathering power of 25, which is good.

Many beginning bird watchers are fooled at first into thinking that power or magnification is most important. They think that if 7 power is good, 10 or 12 power would be better. But this isn't so. First, the average person cannot hold a high-power glass still enough to watch a bird easily. The higher the magnification, the more difficult it is to hold a glass steady in your hands.

Secondly, high-power glasses, to have a relatively high light-gathering ability, need a larger objective lens. Thus the binocular would be large and heavy and bulky. After a day in the field with heavy binoculars, you would wish you had a lighter pair.

In general then, 6 x 30, 7 x 35, or 7 x 50 are the best for bird watching, with 7 x 35 being best for most people.

FIELD

Another thing to watch for in selecting binoculars is *field*. The field is the width covered by the glasses at a given distance. Let's say that the field of a 7 x 35 binocular is 120 feet. This means that at 1000 yards you can see a strip of landscape that is 120 feet wide.

The wider the field, the better the glasses are for bird watching. Frequently you will see birds in flight and want to pick them up with the binoculars quickly before they are out of sight. This is difficult with a narrow field.

METHOD OF FOCUS

Another thing to watch for in binoculars is the method of focus. Some binoculars have central focus and some have individual focus. Central focus means that you can focus both lenses at the same time as a bird flies away from you or toward you—or as you look farther away, or closer—to see birds. This is the best kind to get if you can. But with practice, you can use individual-focus binoculars almost as quickly and easily. Frequently glasses with separately focused lenses are less expensive.

WHERE TO BUY BINOCULARS

When purchasing binoculars, go to a store with a good reputation, an old, established store in your community that you know will stand behind the product it sells.

Now the market in America is flooded with foreign-made binoculars. Some of these glasses are excellent and some are not. But you cannot always know which are good by looking at the glasses. You cannot tell the quality by looking at the glasses, or even through them, unless you are an expert. Sometimes even the experts are fooled.

On the surface a pair of binoculars may look good. They may have an apparently well-made exterior and a good case. But it's the lenses that really count. Sometimes even the lenses seem good, and as long as the glasses are in the showcase, they may be good. But the least jarring may put them out of line, so that when you look through them, the two lenses may show two images that are not lined up. Or the construction may be such that moisture from dampness in the air or from temperature changes seeps in and forms a film between the lenses.

Some of these glasses may even corrode so that they cannot be focused or may literally fall apart after a few months of use. Many of the binoculars you see advertised for $15 to $25 are in this class, but some are not.

Well-established camera or optical shops cannot afford to sell inferior binoculars. They have the binoculars tested scientifically before they sell them. Then if anything goes wrong, you may get the glasses repaired without charge or exchanged for a new pair.

Rugged construction is very important in binoculars used for bird watching. The best plan is to get yours from a reputable dealer and be guided by his advice.

Don't be fooled by magazine or newspaper advertisements of cheap field glasses that are called binoculars and sell for $2.98 or $3.98. They are, in most cases, a waste of money. The difference is this: Field glasses are just a series of lenses in two barrels, mounted rigidly side by side. Generally, 4 power is about tops for good field glasses. The lenses absorb so much light that the light-gathering power is poor. When you look through cheap field glasses, you see two images side by side. With binoculars, prisms on the inside of the barrels reflect the light so that light-gathering power is better. The barrels may be moved so that by looking through them you see one image in three dimensions, as your eyes normally do.

TELESCOPES

Telescopes have an important place in bird watching, especially when you want to see birds that are a long distance away—ducks on a lake, an owl in a tree, or a hawk sitting on a fence post on the other side of a field.

Telescopes generally have a higher power than binoculars, the

Prismatic telescope

power ranging from 10 to 30 or even higher. But the field is much smaller, and most of the time you need a tripod or other support to hold the scope steady.

Telescopes generally are of two kinds: draw-tube or prismatic. The draw-tube scope is the kind you've seen in pictures of old sea captains looking at the horizon for the sail of a ship.

Each tube has its own lenses, and as they are pulled out, the scope may be focused. The scope is closed up for easy carrying. You've probably heard the word *telescope* used as an adjective—*telescoping* legs on a tripod, for example. This refers to the old draw-tube scope, in which the tubes slid one within the other.

The newer scopes are built much like one barrel of binoculars. Within the tube are prisms that reflect the image, and focusing is accomplished by turning the eyepiece in and out a little. Generally these prismatic scopes have better light-gathering power, a wider field, are lighter in weight and easier to use.

Draw-tube telescope on a tripod

BIRD GUIDES

An important piece of equipment for any bird watcher is a good, easy-to-use pocket bird guide. The ones mentioned in the last chapter are the best you can get. The following list will give you an idea of the books you can choose from:

Audubon Bird Guide, Eastern Land Birds, by Richard Pough. Garden City, N. Y., Doubleday & Company, $3.50. Forty-eight color plates of land birds and excellent text cover field marks, habits, song, nest, and range of birds found in the East.

Audubon Bird Guide, Water Birds, by Richard Pough. Garden City, N. Y., Doubleday & Company, $3.50. Similar to above book, but covers water birds.

Audubon Bird Guides, by Richard Pough. Garden City, N. Y., Doubleday & Company, $5.95. Pocket-sized combined edition of *Audubon Bird Guide, Eastern Land Birds* and *Audubon Bird Guide, Water Birds.*

Field Book of Eastern Birds, by Leon Hausman. New York, G. P. Putnam's Sons, $4.50.

Field Guide to the Birds, by Roger Tory Peterson. Boston, Houghton Mifflin Company, $3.75. Probably carried on more bird trips by more people than any other book; 1000 illustrations, 500 in color. Easy-to-read text helpful in identifying birds found east of the Great Plains.

Field Guide to Western Birds, by Roger Tory Peterson. Boston, Houghton Mifflin Company, $3.75. Similar to *Field Guide to the Birds* by the same author, but covering birds found in Montana, Wyoming, Colorado, New Mexico, Western Texas, Utah, Idaho, Washington, Oregon, Nevada, and California.

A Guide to Most Familiar American Birds, by Herbert Zim and Ira Gabrielson. New York, Simon & Schuster, $1.00 paper bound, $1.50 cloth bound. An inexpensive pocket-sized book with color illustrations and text, covering most commonly seen land and water birds.

According to reports, more experienced bird watchers use the Roger Tory Peterson Guide than any other.

"A Guide to the Most Familiar American Birds"

BIRD CALLS

Recently, bird calls that supposedly anyone can use have appeared on the market. The most popular ones are small hollowed-out pieces of wood with a metal plug. As you turn the plug in the tube, you make a squeak or whistle. The speed with which you turn the metal plug and the pressure of the plug against the wood controls the tone, pitch, and volume of the bird call imitation.

These calls have been sold in large numbers, and there are people, the manufacturers especially, who claim all sorts of spectacular results.

You may want to try out one of these calls. They cost only $1.00 or $1.50 and you too may be successful in attracting birds so that you can get a closer look. It's worth a try for the fun of it anyway, but it seems to many bird watchers that these calls are "gadgets" and should not be considered an essential piece of bird watching equipment.

WHAT TO WEAR ON A FIELD TRIP

In bird watching, as in any other outdoor hobby, clothing is important. Good sturdy shoes are probably the most important part of clothing. Since on an average bird hike you may hike through woods and fields, along the edge of a marsh or swamp, through mud or sand, over rough country and smooth, the sturdier the shoes are, the better.

Many experienced bird watchers use "high tops"—shoes that are eight to ten inches high, with composition soles to prevent slipping.

Shoes such as these support your feet and ankles and make walking easier. They keep your feet dry in wet weather, or even in the early morning when the dew is heavy. In sandy country, they keep out sand and make walking more enjoyable. If you plan to do much walking to look for birds, get a good pair of leather hiking boots.

If you plan only an occasional trip, ordinary shoes and overshoes for wet weather will be sufficient. But avoid rubber boots that go directly over your feet. In the course of a day they become quite

Leather hiking boot

uncomfortable, and in cold weather your feet will be cold most of the time.

In any case, use wool socks. Experienced hikers have found that wool socks are much more comfortable, since they absorb perspiration. Two light pairs of wool socks are warmer than a heavy pair, and, in addition, help to prevent blisters.

Any pair of loose-fitting trousers or slacks provide good protection for your legs. Since you may be plodding through briers or brush at times, some tough material is advisable.

Wool shirts and jackets are also helpful to ward off the cold of early morning—or all day in fall or winter. If the wind is blowing, use a parka of tight-woven material or a ski or golf jacket on the outside. This will cut the wind and keep you warm.

Remember that clothing cannot *make* you warm. It can only *keep* you warm. Avoid getting wet from rain or damp from perspiration and you will be warmer.

The nylon ponchos that are now sold for fishermen or hunters are helpful, too, for bird watchers. These ponchos fold up into a pocket-sized package that can be opened quickly to provide protection from a sudden rain or unexpected storm.

No one can have fun watching birds if he is uncomfortable because of the weather. No bird is fun when your feet seem to be freezing, your hands are blue with cold, or the hot sun beats down. Be sure to go out prepared for weather so that you can spend your time enjoying birds. The right kind of clothing makes a lot of difference.

RECORD-KEEPING EQUIPMENT

Very soon after you start bird watching, you will decide to keep records of what you see. You will want to remember what birds you saw, how many of each kind, the date, the weather, and other important information.

At first, probably, a small loose-leaf notebook and automatic pencil will be sufficient (automatic pencil because you don't want to

No.		No.	
	Warbler, Brewster's		Tanager, Scarlet
	Laurence's		Summer
	Bachman's		Cardinal
	Tennessee		Grosbeak, Rose-br.
	Orange-crowned		Blue
	Nashville		Bunting, Indigo
	Parula		Painted
	Yellow		Dickcissel
	Magnolia		Grosbeak, Evening
	Cape May		Finch, Purple
	Bl.-throat. Blue		Grosbeak, Pine
	Myrtle		Redpoll
	Bl.-throat. Green		Siskin, Pine
	Cerulean		Goldfinch
	Blackburnian		Crossbill, Red
	Yellow-throated		White-winged
	Chestnut-sided		Towhee, Red-eyed
	Bay-breasted		White-eyed
	Black-poll		Sparrow, Ipswich
	Pine		Savannah
	Kirtland's		Grasshopper
	Prairie		Leconte's
	Palm		Henslow's
	Yellow Palm		Sharp-tailed
	Oven-bird		Acadian
	Water-Thrush, North.		Nelson's
	Louisiana		Seaside
	Warbler, Kentucky		Dusky
	Connecticut		Vesper
	Mourning		Lark
	Yellow, throat		Pine-wood
	Chat, Yellow-breasted		Bachman's
	Warbler, Hooded		Junco, Slate-colored
	Wilson's		Sparrow, Tree
	Canada		Chipping
	Redstart		Clay-colored
	Sparrow, English		Field
	Bobolink		Harris's
	Meadowlark, Eastern		White-crowned
	Blackbird, Yellow-h.		White-throated
	Red-wing		Fox
	Oriole, Orchard		Lincoln's
	Baltimore		Swamp
	Blackbird, Rusty		Song
	Grackle, Boat-tailed		Longspur, Lapland
	Purple		Smith's
	Bronzed		Bunting, Snow
	Cowbird		

Accidentals...

Total Species.........................Individuals.........................

NATIONAL AUDUBON SOCIETY
1130 Fifth Ave., New York 28, N.Y.
2c each   100 for $1.75

© Copyright 1938, National Audubon Society   Printed in U.S.A.
10M-1-55

AUDUBON
DAILY FIELD CARD
OF
BIRDS
Occurring in North America
EAST OF THE MISSISSIPPI RIVER

Observer..

Locality..

Date.............................Time.............................

Weather.............................Wind.............................

Subspecies, with the exception of a few forms, easily recognizable in the field, are omitted.

Put a more detailed account of today's observations in a separate notebook. Maybe you have seen something new!

No.		No.	
	Loon, Common		Ibis, Wood
	Red-throated		Glossy
	Grebe, Holboell's		White
	Horned		Spoonbill, Roseate
	Pied-billed		Swan, Mute
	Shearwater, Sooty		Whistling
	Greater		Goose, Canada
	Cory's		Brant
	Petrel, Leach's		Goose, White-fronted
	Wilson's		Snow
	Pelican, White		Blue
	Brown		Mallard
	Gannet		Duck, Red-leg. Black
	Cormorant, European		Common Black
	Double-crested		Florida
	Water-Turkey		Gadwall
	Man-o'-war-bird		Widgeon, European
	Heron, Great White		Baldpate
	Great Blue		Pintail
	Egret, American		Teal, European
	Snowy		Green-winged
	Heron, Louisiana		Blue-winged
	Little Blue		Shoveller
	Green		Duck, Wood
	Bl.-crown. Night		Redhead
	Y.-crown. Night		Duck, Ring-necked
	Bittern, American		Canvas back
	Least		Duck, Greater Scaup

have to sharpen a pencil out in the woods if you can avoid it).

Later on, you may want to get printed check lists and record books that are published just for the purpose of keeping bird records. But in Peterson's *Field Guide to the Birds* you will find a check list that you may copy in a notebook as a starter. For a more elaborate record-keeping system write to the National Audubon Society, 1150 Fifth Ave., New York, for a price list and description.

"Audubon Daily Field Card of Birds"

No.		No.		No.		No.	
——	Duck, Lesser Scaup	——	Plover, Cuban Snowy	——	Tern	——	Lark, N. Horned
——	Golden-eye, American	——	Semipalmated	——	Royal	——	Prairie Horned
——	Barrow's	——	Wilson's	——	Cabot's	——	Swallow, Tree
——	Buffle-head	——	Killdeer	——	Caspian	——	Bank
——	Old-squaw	——	Golden	——	Black	——	Rough-winged
——	Duck, Harlequin	——	Black-bellied	——	Noddy	——	Barn
——	Eider, American	——	Turnstone, Ruddy	——	Skimmer, Black	——	Cliff
——	King	——	Woodcock	——	Auk, Razor-billed	——	Martin, Purple
——	Scoter, White-winged	——	Snipe, Wilson's	——	Murre, Atlantic	——	Jay, Canada
——	Surf	——	Curlew, Long-billed	——	Brunnich's	——	Blue
——	American	——	Hudsonian	——	Dovekie	——	Florida
——	Duck, Ruddy	——	Plover, Upland	——	Guillemot, Black	——	Raven
——	Merganser, Hooded	——	Sandpiper, Spotted	——	Puffin, Atlantic	——	Crow
——	American	——	Solitary	——	Pigeon, White-cr.	——	Fish
——	Red-breasted	——	Willet	——	Dove, Rock	——	Chickadee, Black-c.
——	Vulture, Turkey	——	Yellow-legs, Greater	——	Mourning	——	Carolina
——	Black	——	Lesser	——	Ground	——	Brown-c.
——	Kite, Swallow-tailed	——	Knot	——	Cuckoo, Maynard's	——	Titmouse, Tufted
——	Mississippi	——	Sandpiper, Purple	——	Yellow-billed	——	Nuthatch, White-br.
——	Everglade	——	Pectoral	——	Black-billed	——	Red-breasted
——	Goshawk	——	White-rumped	——	Owl, Barn	——	Brown-headed
——	Hawk, Sharp-shinned	——	Baird's	——	Screech	——	Creeper, Brown
——	Cooper's	——	Least	——	Great Horned	——	Wren, House
——	Red-tailed	——	Red-backed	——	Snowy	——	Winter
——	Red-shouldered	——	Dowitcher, Eastern	——	Hawk	——	Bewick's
——	Broad-winged	——	Long-billed	——	Burrowing	——	Carolina
——	Short-tailed	——	Sandpiper, Stilt	——	Barred	——	Long-bill. Marsh
——	Rough-legged	——	Semipalmated	——	Great Gray	——	Short-bill. Marsh
——	Eagle, Golden	——	Western	——	Long-eared	——	Mockingbird
——	Bald	——	Buff-breasted	——	Short-eared	——	Catbird
——	Hawk, Marsh	——	Godwit, Marbled	——	Richardson's	——	Thrasher, Brown
——	Osprey	——	Hudsonian	——	Saw-whet	——	Robin
——	Caracara, Audubon's	——	Sanderling	——	Chuck-will's-widow	——	Thrush, Wood
——	Gyrfalcon	——	Stilt, Black-necked	——	Whip-poor-will	——	Hermit
——	Hawk, Duck	——	Phalarope, Red	——	Nighthawk	——	Olive-backed
——	Pigeon	——	Wilson's	——	Swift, Chimney	——	Gray-cheeked
——	Sparrow	——	Northern	——	Hummingbird, R.-thr.	——	Veery
——	Grouse, Spruce	——	Jaeger, Pomarine	——	Kingfisher, Belted	——	Bluebird
——	Ruffed	——	Parasitic	——	Flicker	——	Gnatcatcher, Blue-g.
——	Ptarmigan, Willow	——	Long-tailed	——	Woodpecker, Pileated	——	Kinglet, Golden-cr.
——	Rock	——	Skua	——	Red-bellied	——	Ruby-crowned
——	Chicken, Prairie	——	Gull, Glaucous	——	Red-headed	——	Pipit, American
——	Grouse, Sharp-t.	——	Iceland	——	Sapsucker, Yellow-b.	——	Waxwing, Bohemian
——	Partridge, European	——	Kumlien's	——	Woodpecker, Hairy	——	Cedar
——	Bob-white	——	Great Black-backed	——	Downy	——	Shrike, Northern
——	Pheasant, Ring-n.	——	Herring	——	Red-cockaded	——	Loggerhead
——	Turkey	——	Ring-billed	——	Arc. Three-toed	——	Starling
——	Crane, Sandhill	——	Laughing	——	Am. Three-toed	——	Vireo, White-eyed
——	Limpkin	——	Franklin's	——	Ivory-billed	——	Yellow-throated
——	Rail, King	——	Bonaparte's	——	Kingbird, Eastern	——	Blue-headed
——	Clapper	——	Little	——	Gray	——	Black-whiskered
——	Virginia	——	Kittiwake	——	Arkansas	——	Red-eyed
——	Sora	——	Gull, Sabine's	——	Flycatcher, Crested	——	Philadelphia
——	Rail, Yellow	——	Tern, Gull-billed	——	Phoebe	——	Warbling
——	Black	——	Forster's	——	Flycatcher, Yellow-b.	——	Warbler, Bl. and Wh.
——	Gallinule, Purple	——	Common	——	Acadian	——	Prothonotary
——	Florida	——	Arctic	——	Alder	——	Swainson's
——	Coot	——	Roseate	——	Least	——	Worm-eating
——	Oyster-catcher	——	Sooty	——	Pewee, Wood	——	Golden-winged
——	Plover, Piping	——	Least	——	Flycatcher, Olive-s.	——	Blue-winged

Start out early in your bird watching career to keep good notes on what you see.

Every experienced outdoorsman has a few items he carries in his pockets just in case he needs them. Oldtime bird watchers are no exception, especially on all-day trips or hikes.

Some of these items include: a sharp pocketknife; a small com-

Reverse side of "Audubon Daily Field Card of Birds"

pass; waterproofed matches; some Band-Aids for blisters or scratches (drugstore, $.25); a snake-bite kit in poisonous snake country; a bottle of insect repellent for mosquitoes (drugstore, $.50); some candy bars or other snack for lunch, and perhaps a small pack for collecting unusual shells, rocks, or other things found along the way.

Audubon Birdfile Card

COMMON LOON   Gavia immer immer

MY LIFE LIST NUMBER _____

MY LOCAL LIST NUMBER _____

MIGRATION DATA (SPRING)

YEAR	1ST SEEN	LOCATION	NUMBER	WAVE DATE*	LOCATION	NUMBER	LAST SEEN	LOCATION	NUMBER

NESTING DATA

YEAR	LOCATION	MALE ON TERRITORY	DATE NEST BUILT	NESTING SITE	DATE AND NO. EGGS LAID	DATE HATCH	DATE YOUNG FLY

MIGRATION DATA (FALL) THIS SECTION MAY BE USED FOR WINTER VISITANTS.

YEAR	1ST SEEN	LOCATION	NUMBER	WAVE DATE*	LOCATION	NUMBER	LAST SEEN	LOCATION	NUMBER

*WAVE DATE—DAY OF HIGHEST COUNT DURING MIGRATION OR SEASON.

BIRDFILE

Chapter Four

BIRD WATCHING TECHNIQUES

Successful bird watching requires a few special techniques that you will probably discover for yourself rather quickly after your first few trips afield. But learning by experience is the difficult way if you can benefit from the experience of someone else.

When you first think about it, you may think that all you have to do is to go out and look at birds. But remember that you really want to see that bird as closely as possible and in the best possible light so that you may study the color, all the markings, and see firsthand what the bird is doing.

HOW TO GET A GOOD LOOK AT A BIRD

Let's suppose that you are walking along the edge of a field. You hear a bird and look up. There it is on a fence post fifty yards away. You lift up your binoculars and take a look. The bird seems to be all black. You must get a closer look to pick out distinctive markings and any color that is there.

First, though, look to see where the sun is. Are you looking into the sun? Is the bird between you and the sun? That's the reason that you can't see color or distinctive markings. All you see is a silhouette, and it's difficult to tell what kind of a bird it is.

Now take a long detour and walk around the bird so you will be on the other side. When the sun shines from behind you on the bird, you'll get a much better view. But be careful. Don't frighten it. Walk slowly and a long way around.

Now you can see some color. The bird's breast seems yellowish. Its back is brownish. There's a black V on its neck. You know it's a meadow lark, but how about a closer look? When you get much closer, in spring, you can see the bright yellow of the lark and yellow-and-white stripes over the eye.

The time has come to "stalk" the bird, to get as close to it as you can without making it fly away. Stalking takes a little practice, but it is quite easy. Walk very slowly, a little way at a time, then stop for a few seconds or a minute. Walk a few feet closer, then stop. Keep watching the bird. You will see that it is probably watching you at the same time.

If it seems uneasy or jittery, stop and wait till it calms down. Then walk a little closer. Do not make any sudden movements. Lift your binoculars slowly and carefully. Easy does it. You should be able to approach within fifty feet or so before the bird flies. But in the meantime you will be able to see the color and stripes very well and memorize the features of the bird so you know it the next time you see it.

Oriole:

Beak

WHEN TO WATCH BIRDS

Generally, early morning and late afternoon or early evening are the best times to watch birds. Early morning is best of all, for then birds are hungry after the long night and are actively looking for food.

Birds are such active creatures that they burn up a lot of energy. They need lots of food to keep them alive. During the spring nesting season they have to hunt for food most of the time to keep the young birds fed. Early in the morning they are especially active and therefore easier to see.

During the middle of the day they usually find a safe place to rest—a place, frequently, where they are sheltered and out of sight of their natural enemies. During spring and fall migrations, sometimes, you can see them any time of day. During the winter, too, if you have placed feeders out in your yard (see pp. 61-69), you may see birds any time you look. But generally early morning is the best time to watch.

Wing

Tail

Leg

BEST PLACES TO LOOK FOR BIRDS

After a little experience on bird hikes, you'll find that you can pick out places where you will find birds rather easily. Usually these best places will be the edges of woods, marshes, ponds, or fields; road-sides; places along the beach where the water laps the shore.

There's a good reason for it, too. Wherever two kinds of natural area—field, forest, swamp, or lake—touch each other, you'll find a larger variety of plant life. This variety of plant life is attractive to animals, and especially to birds.

Usually in these "edges" there will be dense brush, briers, or undergrowth, places where birds can hide from their enemies and find shelter from heat or cold. In these edges, too, in the variety of plants, will be more food for birds, either fruit, or seeds, or insects that are attracted by the plants found there.

It's true that you will find birds out in the middle of a field, or in the center of a lake, or in the middle of a forest. But the variety will almost always be less, especially in spring or summer, than along the edges.

Just as in an apartment house where some people live on the ground floor and others at different levels up to the top floor, in the woods birds feed or nest at different levels from the ground up to the tops of the trees.

When you know these things and find them out for yourself, you can almost tell at a glance when a certain spot is worth looking over for birds.

Sewing a four-inch seam at the end of the muslin. Note buttonholes

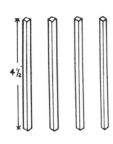

Upright legs of the bird blind

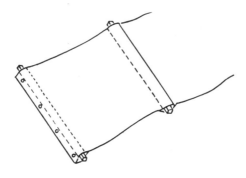

The upright legs inserted in the muslin

BIRD BLIND

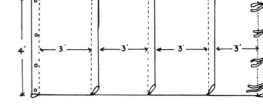

The muslin, ready for insertion of the upright legs

FAVORITE BIRD WATCHING SPOTS

After a while, too, you'll find a few "hot spots" in your area where you almost always seem to find interesting birds. If there's a bird club near by, ask some of the members to show you some of these spots. The best places may be small groves of pines on a golf course or along a roadside; the brush or bramble patch on the edge of a marsh; a tangle of honeysuckle growing over an old fence; a fence-row of shrubs and trees between two fields; the shrubs and trees growing along the edges of a stream; even a tangle out in your own yard or in the neighboring park.

In the vicinity of most large cities are dozens of such places where you can be sure of finding from one to a dozen other bird watchers on almost any weekend. Right this minute, if it is daylight and the weather is not too bitter, you could be sure of seeing birds and bird watchers in at least one of these places in or near New York City: Van Cortlandt Park, Prospect Park, Central Park, Riis Park, Rockaway Jetty, Atlantic Beach Jetty, Jones Beach, Bayside Bay, Millneck Pond, or Alley Pond Park.

That's only an example—there are similar places everywhere to look for interesting birds. The more you visit these places and get to know them, the more you will see and the more fun bird watching will be. If you don't know of any bird clubs or of any bird watchers in your area, there is a good book which you can buy or read in your library that will get you started. Look for *A Guide to Bird Finding East of the Mississippi*, by Olin S. Pettingill (New York, Oxford University Press, $6.50) if you live in the east, or *A Guide*

BIRD WATCHING TECHNIQUES

43

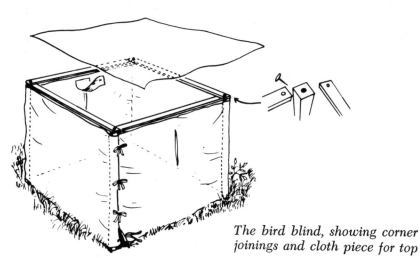

The bird blind, showing corner joinings and cloth piece for top

Using the finished bird blind

to Bird Finding West of the Mississippi, by the same author (New York, Oxford University Press, $6.00) if you live in the east.

Another suggestion is to visit your nearest natural history museum and ask the help of someone in the bird department.

HOW TO BUILD A BIRD BLIND

Perhaps instead of trying to find many different birds, you would like to find out as much as you can about one particular bird or pair of birds. Suppose you found a song sparrow's nest in a rosebush out in your yard, or a robin's nest, or a catbird's nest. If the nest is close enough so you can watch it from a window, you are indeed fortunate. But it may not be so easy to watch, and then you will have to build what bird watchers call a "blind."

The purpose of the blind is to hide you so the bird will not see you and become frightened. When the bird cannot see you, it will carry on its regular habits—and with the blind you can be only a few feet away, watching everything that happens.

If you already have some kind of a tent, perhaps you can make it do as a blind. If not, it's easy to make one.

The material required is: 4 pieces of wood 2 inches x 4½ feet long or 4 poles about 2 inches in diameter and 4½ feet long; some unbleached muslin 4 feet wide and 15 feet long; needles and heavy thread.

In one end of the cloth sew a seam 4 inches wide. At the top, in the middle, and at the bottom of the seam make buttonholes.

Three feet from the end seam sew a "loop" or seam that is 4 inches wide. Three feet farther on sew another loop or seam 4 inches wide, sew a third loop another 3 feet along. In the other end of the cloth sew a 2-inch seam and three 10-inch-long tie strings that fit into the buttonholes in the opposite end.

Slide the four pieces of wood or poles into the four 4-inch loops and slide a 1-inch dowel or piece of bamboo through the 2-inch seam.

Next, set the blind upright on the ground in the shape of a square. Tie the strings through the buttonholes and around the upright leg.

Quail:

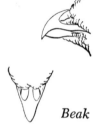

Beak

Wing

Tail

Leg

When the blind is set up and forms a square, measure the exact distance from leg one to leg two, from leg two to leg three, from leg three to leg four, and from four to one, going clockwise around the square. Cut pieces of wood 1 x 2 inches (shingle lath) the same length as the distance between the legs. These pieces will act as crosspieces and will keep the blind from collapsing. The crosspiece should fit exactly across the tops of the legs.

Next drill a ¼-inch hole in the top of each leg and through the crosspiece about ½-inch in from the end. Then you can push a nail through the crosspiece and into the end of the leg to hold them in place.

You will need a piece of cloth for the top, which should be the same material as the sides. Cut it slightly larger than the top and fasten to the crosspieces with thumbtacks, or pull it over the sides and fasten it with safety pins.

Finally cut slits in two sides of the blind, to look through. Sew a piece of cloth over each slit on the inside so that it hangs over the slit when not in use. When you want to look through the opening, hold up the cover with a safety pin.

HOW TO USE THE BLIND

When you get your blind set near a bird feeder, pond edge, nest, or other suitable place, be sure that the cloth is stretched tight and that there are no loose pieces to flap in the breeze. Nothing will frighten birds more quickly.

You may want to camouflage the blind somehow, such as by covering it with grass, boughs, or branches. This cover will help it blend into the background and be less visible to birds.

Then walk around the blind and see if you can see through it. If you can, a bird can, and your movements may frighten it. If you can see through it, cover up the point where light passes through.

Crawl inside the blind and make yourself comfortable. Open the peephole and focus your glasses on the nest or feeder or other place where you expect birds to be. You will be in for many interesting minutes, especially if young birds are in the nest.

WHAT TO WATCH FOR

Whether you watch birds from a blind or from a hiding place behind a tree or bush, there are several things to look for that are interesting.

If you are watching birds building a nest, find out whether the male or the female builds the nest or whether they work on it together. When the nest is built, watch to see which bird incubates (hatches) the egg. Perhaps they will take turns, or perhaps the female will spend most of the time on the nest while the male flits around near by.

You may be interested in finding out how many eggs are in the nest and how long it takes them to hatch.

Most songbirds when hatched are nearly naked and helpless. The parent birds must feed them and care for them for about two weeks. You may be interested in finding out how long it takes for the young birds to leave the nest and how many days pass after they hatch until they can fly.

You certainly will be interested in watching the adult birds feed the young, which always seem to be hungry and ready to eat. The parents are busy all day long from dawn to dusk hunting for soft-bodied grubs and soft insects to push down the yawning throats of their young. Try to discover what kinds of insects the birds feed their young.

Then count how many insects they bring back to the nest each time they return. Next count the number of times they return in an hour. Figuring that a bird feeds its young for ten or twelve hours a day, you can determine how many insects a young bird devours in two weeks.

BIRD MIGRATION

After the lull of late summer has passed, the bird watcher is in for another busy season. For during the fall a great many birds will be passing through on their way south.

Why birds fly south every winter and north again every spring is one of the great mysteries of nature. There are several theories on

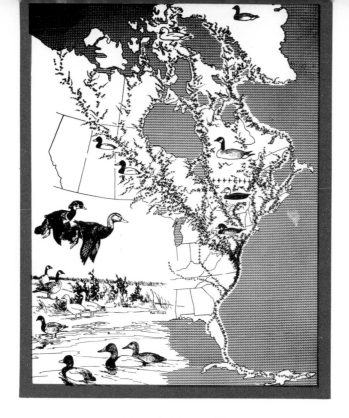

Map of Atlantic Flyway

Map of Central Flyway

Map of Mississippi Flyway

Map of Pacific Flyway

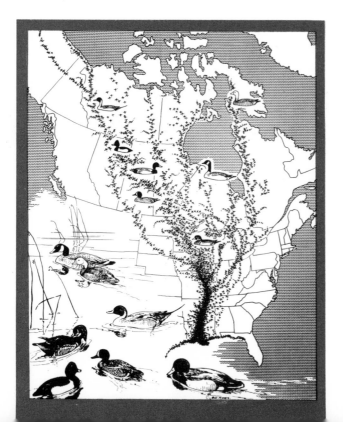

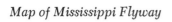

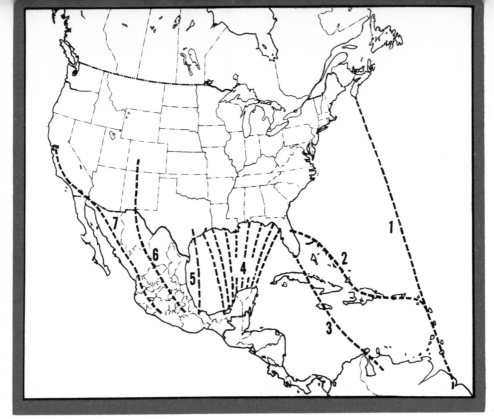

Principal migration routes used by birds in passing from North America to winter quarters in the West Indies, Central America and South America.

why birds migrate, all of which are reasonable explanations. But scientists are not yet sure that they know the exact reason.

One theory of migration goes all the way back to the glacier that came down from the north thousands of years ago. As the weather grew colder due to the glacier, and snow and ice covered everything, birds had to move south ahead of it in order to find food. Some went farther than others—all the way to central South America. As the glacier retreated, the birds again came north.

Another theory is that in spring the increase of light from the sun stimulates the birds to fly north. It also stimulates them to mate, nest, and raise their young.

A third reason given for bird migration, or seasonal movement from one area to another, is the search for food. Snow and ice and cold weather cover seeds and fruits which some birds seek for food.

Winter also sends insects into the ground or under bark, where they are difficult to find. Small animals crawl into holes in the ground and sleep all winter, and birds that would normally eat them must move south in search of other food.

But whatever the reason for bird migration, it is still one of the most interesting things in nature. If you want to read more about it, see Chapter 10, which contains a list of books about birds.

WHERE TO WATCH FOR MIGRATING BIRDS

As birds migrate, they generally follow well-defined landmarks, mountain ranges, rivers, sea coasts, or valleys. This will give a helpful hint as to where to watch for migrating birds. If you live near the coast, look along the beaches and coastal marshes. Visit any points of land that jut out into the ocean. You will probably see hawks, owls, shore birds, ducks, and geese in considerable numbers, as well as smaller birds that follow the coastline south.

If you live near mountain ranges or in a river valley, you have an excellent chance to watch migration. Find a particularly good place where there seems to be a great many birds. There may be a good food supply there, or shelter where birds may roost on their way south.

In the mountains of Pennsylvania, there is one spot called Hawk Mountain, so named because of the vast number of hawks that can be seen there during the fall migration. Hawk Mountain is now a bird sanctuary, to which bird watchers go each fall to see large numbers of hawks, eagles and vultures on their southward flights.

If you live on one of the major duck flyways, you will be able to see great numbers of ducks. Pitch a blind near a pond or marsh and watch ducks as they stop to feed and rest.

The maps on page 47 shows the major flyways used by birds in their long migrations. You may be interested, in watching birds that fly south through your area, to see by your map how far south they go after leaving you.

Many of the ducks you see will winter along the coastal areas

"A Field Guide to Animal Tracks."

of southern United States. Warblers will fly to Central and South America. Bobolinks go all the way to central South America, as do many of the shore birds—sandpipers and plovers.

By reading about the birds you see, you will be able to chart their route south on a map and see for yourself what long distances they travel—and remember that they do not have radar equipment or any of the navigational helps that airplanes use. As you read about migration, you will certainly agree that it is one of the most interesting things in all nature.

WHAT BIRD TRACKS CAN TELL YOU

There are several things you can tell about birds just by looking at their tracks. First, you can tell something of the size of the bird—large birds have large feet and vice versa. But more than that, you can tell whether the bird is a swimmer; whether it wades in mud and shallow water searching for food; whether it walks or whether it hops.

Birds that swim a large part of the time, such as ducks and gulls, have webbed feet, and you can tell this by the impression in the mud or sand. Wading birds such as herons or egrets have quite large feet and long toes to keep them from sinking in the soft mud. Hopping birds such as sparrows leave tracks in pairs—as you would if you placed your feet side by side and hopped through some soft dirt. Birds such as grackles or cowbirds leave tracks one after the other, showing that they walk.

Generally you can assume that hopping birds usually spend more time in trees and shrubbery searching for food, while walking birds feed on the ground, though this is not always true.

If you are interested in bird tracks, you might want to read *A Field Guide to Animal Tracks,* by Olaus Murie (Boston, Houghton Mifflin Company, $3.75).

Once you start taking hikes in the woods or short trips to the park, it won't take long to learn how to watch birds and how to understand what you see. The more skilled you become, the more fun you'll have watching wild birds.

Tracks of three wild turkey gobblers on beach

Chapter Five

HOW TO BUILD BIRDHOUSES

WHY BIRDHOUSES ARE NECESSARY

Strange as it may seem, many birds have no place to nest just because people are too neat. It works like this: Birds such as bluebirds, chickadees, woodpeckers, flickers, tree swallows, crested flycatchers, screech owls, and other birds nest in holes in trees. But when trees die in our yards, parks, or wooded areas, we cut them down. We just do not like to see dead trees. Our neatness means that some birds have fewer homes, and since these birds will nest nowhere else except in holes in trees, or in bird boxes, frequently the birds become quite rare in some localities as nesting species.

Building and setting out bird boxes is easy, and it's fun. More than that, it may well be responsible for increasing the number of certain birds which have been rare in your area.

A few years ago, a Boy Scout troop in Erie County, New York, was directly responsible for a huge increase in the number of bluebirds in the area. They did it first by building and setting out more than 150 bluebird houses—and then by cleaning out and repairing the houses each fall after the birds had left.

On Cape Cod, Massachusetts, another group of boys was successful in getting tree swallows to nest where previously they had not been known except as migrants passing through. Again the secret was building and setting out suitable nesting boxes.

WHERE TO PUT BIRDHOUSES

Bird boxes may be put up almost anywhere, and it is amazing how quickly they will attract occupants. A few years ago, a fellow working on a Boy Scout Merit Badge looked for a place to set out some

Martins and house

FLOWER POT BIRDHOUSE

GOURD BIRDHOUSE

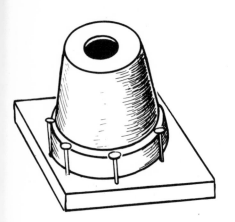

The finished flower pot birdhouse

The flower pot birdhouse in use

The gourd birdhouse in use

The finished gourd birdhouse

nesting boxes. He lived in the middle of a large city where there wasn't even a suitable park. One day he passed a cemetery and saw that there were lots of trees there and that it was apparently a good place for birds if they had places to nest. The cemetery officials readily gave permission for the birdhouses, and he set them out. Out of eighteen houses, ten were used the first year, by house wrens, chickadees, and downy woodpeckers. One starling family took over one house, and English sparrows occupied two.

In other places, the rows of trees between the fairways on golf courses have been used successfully for birdhouses, and in the more open country, fence posts along roadsides, trees in apple orchards, and posts or trees along the edge of woodlots or hedgerows. There are many places where birdhouses may be set out—but most important are the specifications of the houses themselves.

Log house with removable front

EASY-TO-CLEAN BIRDHOUSES

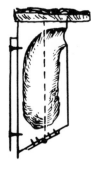

Wooden house with removable top

Cross-section of rustic house showing hollowed-out cavity

Log house with removable top

GENERAL REQUIREMENTS OF SUCCESSFUL BIRDHOUSES

Cities, villages, towns, and counties frequently have building codes that set forth how houses for human occupants must be built. Certain specifications must be met before the houses may be occupied. These codes are designed to protect the safety of the people who live in the houses. Birds themselves have certain requirements for their homes or they will not move in. Then, too, other requirements must be met for the protection of the birds.

Building bird boxes may be a complete waste of time, money, and energy if, after the houses are built, birds will not use them, or if they do use them but do not successfully raise a crop of young.

Here are some general rules to follow:

1. Make the houses for specific birds—wood duck boxes, chickadee boxes, bluebird houses. Do not just make "birdhouses."

MARTIN HOUSE

Side view

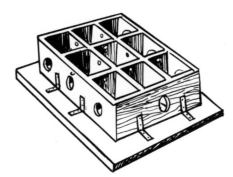

Single story with roof removed

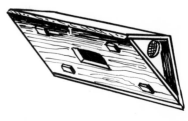

Finished roof before assembling

Bluebird house

Wren house

Nuthatch house

2. Do not try apartment houses, except for martins. Most birds demand privacy and will drive away others who come too close to their houses.

3. Make the holes to fit the bird. Every bird has its own requirements. With songbird houses, English sparrows or starlings will move in and drive away more desirable birds if the hole is large enough. With wood duck boxes, raccoons may get in and destroy the eggs or young ducks if the hole is not just right.

4. Do not use tin cans as a general rule. The sun beating down may heat up the inside like an oven and bake the young birds.

5. Do not set up too many houses in a small area. As a general rule, three or four to an acre is the largest number that will be used.

6. Do not hide the houses in dense foliage. They should be placed in open shade, on poles, tree trunks, or suspended from branches.

7. Clean out the houses after each season. Birds demand clean houses each year. This means that boxes should have provisions for easy cleaning. Either the tops or bottoms should be hinged or fastened with an easily removable screw so that they may be cleaned without taking them down.

8. All houses should be made so that they are well ventilated and easily drained of any rain water that may blow in. Slits under the roof provide ventilation, and a few holes drilled in the bottom will provide drainage.

Rustic birdhouse with removable front.

Rustic birdhouse with top held by two hooks.

Rustic birdhouse with simple hinged top.

BIRDHOUSE SPECIFICATIONS FOR COMMON SPECIES

Following are specifications for houses for some of the more common species, recommended by the U. S. Department of Agriculture:

Birdhouse Specifications

BLUEBIRD

FLOOR SIZE 5″ x 5″
HEIGHT 8″
HOLE ABOVE FLOOR 6″
DIAMETER OF HOLE 1½″
ABOVE GROUND 5-15′

Place houses in sunny places, in orchard or along roadsides.

CHICKADEE
NUTHATCH
TITMOUSE
DOWNY WOODPECKER

FLOOR SIZE 4″ x 4″
HEIGHT 8-10″
HOLE ABOVE FLOOR 6-8″
DIAMETER OF HOLE 1¼″
ABOVE GROUND 5-15′

These birds prefer a bark-covered house. Use slab wood with bark on it. For woodpeckers place some wood chips in the bottom.

SCREECH OWL

FLOOR SIZE 8″ x 10″
HEIGHT 12-15″
HOLE ABOVE FLOOR 10″
DIAMETER OF HOLE 3¼″
ABOVE GROUND 10-30′

Rustic house is best, but even then you are lucky to get an owl to use it. It is well worth the effort to get one of these interesting birds to nest near your home.

FLICKER

FLOOR SIZE 7″ x 7″
HEIGHT 8″
HOLE ABOVE FLOOR 6″
DIAMETER OF HOLE 3″
ABOVE GROUND 8-20′

Make house of wood at least an inch thick. Sprinkle chips or shavings inside.

HOUSE WREN

FLOOR SIZE 4″ x 4″
HEIGHT 6-8″
HOLE ABOVE FLOOR 6″
DIAMETER OF HOLE 1″
ABOVE GROUND 5-10′

TREE SWALLOW

FLOOR SIZE 5″ x 5″
HEIGHT 6″
HOLE ABOVE FLOOR 5″
DIAMETER OF HOLE 1½″
ABOVE GROUND 5-15′

Place these houses in the open on a post or dead tree, preferably near water.

CRESTED FLYCATCHER

FLOOR SIZE 6″ x 6″
HEIGHT 8-10″
HOLE ABOVE FLOOR 6-8″
DIAMETER OF HOLE 2″
ABOVE GROUND 8-20′

HOW TO MAKE A BASIC BIRD BOX

One of the best all-around bird boxes can be made rather quickly. Here's how to do it:

Use 1-inch thick wood, which is ¾ to ⅞ of an inch thick, as you get it from the lumber yard. Use brass screws and hinges so they will not rust.

To make one house, you will need a piece of wood 6 inches wide (about 5¾ inches as it comes from the mill) and 52 inches long. Saw off a piece 14 inches long for the backboard. Saw off a second piece 5 inches long for the top and cut it down to 5 x 5¼ inches.

Then ripsaw the board for 19 inches so you have a piece 4 inches wide. Cut this piece into two 9½-inch pieces for the sides. Saw a ½-inch triangle off each side so the top will slant toward the front.

Next, rip the board so you have a piece 3¼ inches wide. Cut off a piece 9 inches long for the front and a piece 3¼ inches square for the bottom. The bottom and the front fit inside the sides. Center the sides on the backboard and use screws to fasten in place. Use a hinge to attach the top to the backboard. Be careful drilling the hole so as not to split the front. With a 1½-inch hole, this box is suitable for bluebirds or tree swallows. With a 1-inch hole, it would do for a house wren. Different sizes will make it suitable for different birds.

STANDARD BIRD HOUSE

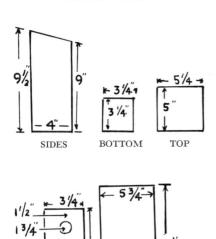

The parts of the bird-house, showing dimensions

The finished bird house in use

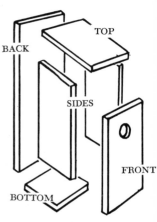

How the parts of the birdhouse fit together

WOOD DUCK BOXES

The general principles for building wood duck boxes are the same as for any bird box. But the size specifications are much larger:

Floor area . . . . 10 x 10 inches
Height of house . . . . 28 inches
Hole diameter . . . . 3 x 5 inches (oval shaped)
Hole above floor . . . . 20 inches
Height above ground . . . . 6 to 20 feet

House may be placed on pole which has been driven into mud in bottom of lake or pond or in trees near water's edge. *Very important:* Place 4 inches of sawdust in the house, and tack screening or hardware cloth inside the front so the young ducks can climb up to the hole.

If the houses are placed on poles, tack sheet metal or tin around the pole for 12 to 20 inches under the house so raccoons cannot climb up and get at the eggs or young birds.

Select a marshy or brushy area so ducks can feed and rest on the water in a protected place. Place the boxes above possible floodwater height.

WOOD DUCK BOX

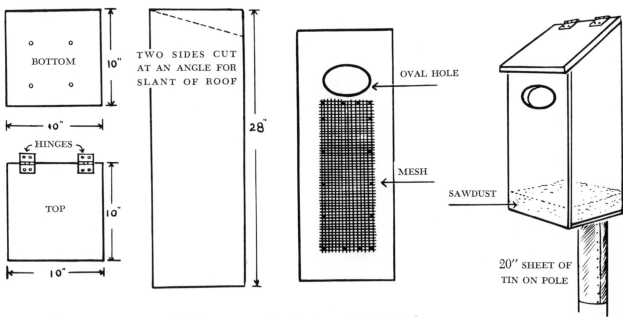

The parts of the wood duck box, showing dimensions   *Inside view of the finished front before assembling*   *The finished wood duck box*

HOW TO BUILD A NESTING-MATERIAL BOX

Some birds will not nest in birdhouses, but nevertheless you can help them. Make a rack, as shown, and fill it with bits of string, yarn, pieces of grass, moss, or other materials that birds such as robins, orioles, thrashers, and catbirds will use in nest-building.

To make such a rack, use wood ¼ by 2 inches wide. Cut two strips 10 inches long and two pieces 6 inches long. Nail them together so that you have a 2-inch deep box without top or bottom. Tack fine-mesh hardware cloth on the box to form a top and bottom. Or you may use a long piece of wire and wrap it around the box several times to form a grill over the open sides.

Then fill the box with nesting materials and hang it in a tree or from a post where birds can get at it and pick out the pieces of string or yarn. When you fill the box, be sure that the string or yarn is in short pieces, 6 to 8 inches long.

Part of the fun comes from watching birds pull out the string and carry it to their nests. But the real fun comes in the fall when you take down the old nest and examine it carefully. If the string or yarn is of different colors or of different kinds, you'll be able to follow one piece through the complicated weaving job that the bird does and see exactly how it made the nest.

HOOK EYE

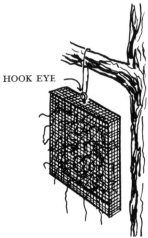

The finished nesting material box in use

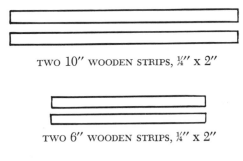

TWO 10″ WOODEN STRIPS, ¼″ x 2″

TWO 6″ WOODEN STRIPS, ¼″ x 2″

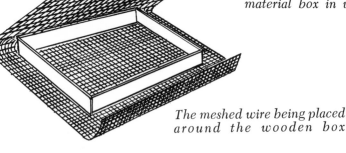

The meshed wire being placed around the wooden box

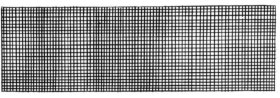

MESHED WIRE

The parts of the nesting material box, showing dimensions

Pieces of wool, string, yarn, grass and moss, cut from 6 to 8 inches long

NESTING MATERIAL BOX

HOW TO HELP ROBINS AND PHOEBES BUILD A HOME

Robins will not nest in birdhouses, but they will nest sometimes on a bracket or shelf set up in a tree. The illustration shows how to make a robin bracket.

Use wood from the ends of an old apple crate, or any other wood that is about an inch thick and 6 inches wide. Cut one piece 6 inches long for a base; a piece 8 inches long for the back; and a piece 8 inches long for the roof. Nail the back to the floor and then nail on the roof so it slants downward slightly toward the front. Use pieces of wood ½ x 2 inches to make a lip around the floor and to support the roof.

Place this bracket 10 to 15 feet up in a tree and fasten it securely.

Phoebes are birds that frequently nest under bridges. They will build their nests up against the rafters or stringers of wooden bridges or even on the ledge of I-beams on steel bridges.

But in many places they will nest up under the eaves of a house or garage if a suitable spot is available. Generally, all that is necessary is a 4- to 6-inch wide board fastened to the house or garage up close to the eaves. Since phoebes nest early and raise two or three broods of young each year, you may have a lot of fun watching them if you are successful in attracting them.

The robin house assembled, and ready for use

ANGLE IRON

A phoebe house under a rafter

PHOEBE HOUSE

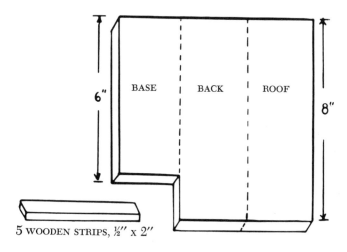

6"

BASE   BACK   ROOF

8"

5 WOODEN STRIPS, ½" x 2"

The parts of the robin house, showing dimensions

ROBIN HOUSE

EASY-TO-MAKE BIRD BOXES

One of the easiest birdhouses to make, if you have an old flowerpot or can get one, is this: Use a clay flowerpot that is about 8 inches in diameter and about 8 inches deep, with a 1-inch hole in the bottom. Get a square piece of board about an inch larger than the open end of the pot.

Lay the board on the floor and place the open end of the flowerpot on the board. Get some nails just long enough to go from the ridge around the pot halfway through the board.

Carefully hammer about six nails into the board around the pot so the heads of the nails catch on the ridge and hold the pot tightly against the board.

Hang this pot on a fence post, clothespole, or tree trunk. House wrens have been attracted to this sort of house.

Florists sometimes sell large gourds, or perhaps you've grown some in your own garden. The gourds must be dry to work right.

Carefully cut a hole of the right size for the bird you want in the gourd, which should be at least 6 inches in diameter. Hang the gourd in a tree with a piece of wire. Wrens, crested flycatchers, and swallows have used gourds for nesting boxes.

Building birdhouses and putting them out is fun in itself. But it's nothing compared with the fun of watching the adult birds carry nesting material into the house and later carry food to their young. Then comes the most fun of all—the day when the young birds poke their heads out of the hole and finally flutter out to learn to fly.

If you build birdhouses this year and expect birds to use them again next year, be sure to clean them out. Remove all of the old nesting material and be sure they are dry and clean before you close them up again. You don't like an untidy or dirty house—neither do birds.

Martins and house

Chapter Six

HOW TO BUILD BIRD FEEDERS

For many bird watchers, winter is the most interesting time of year. During the late fall and winter it is possible to attract many different birds right to your own yard. During the winter, too, if you have patience enough, you may even get birds to feed right from your hand.

Generally, the birds that will visit your yard in the winter are of two kinds: those that eat seeds and those that eat insects. What this means is that seeds of various kinds in feeders will attract the seed eaters and suet will be eaten by the insect eaters.

WHAT TO FEED BIRDS

The following chart will serve as a guide to the kind of feed to put out for different birds:

WINTER FOODS	BIRDS THAT MAY BE ATTRACTED
Mixed seeds (hemp, millet, kaffir corn, cracked corn, etc.)	Cowbird; grackle; redwing; fox, white-throated, tree, song, field and vesper sparrows; catbird; brown thrasher; hermit thrush; purple and house finches; pine siskin; goldfinch.
Sunflower seeds	Evening and pine grosbeaks; cardinal; goldfinch; chickadee; nuthatch; purple finch; blue jay.
Cut up pieces of fruit (apples, banana, etc.), wild fruit such as bayberry, currants	California and brown thrashers; robin; hermit thrush; catbird; bluebird; downy, hairy, and redheaded woodpeckers; flicker; myrtle warbler.

Suet	Downy and hairy woodpeckers; red-breasted and white-breasted nuthatches; chickadee; flicker; tufted titmouse; blue jay; brown creeper; some sparrows; golden-crowned kinglet; red-winged blackbird.
Peanut butter, nutmeats	White-breasted nuthatch, downy woodpecker, chickadee, blue jay, tree and fox sparrows; tufted titmouse; house and purple finches; pine and evening grosbeaks; cardinal; catbird.
Breadcrumbs, doughnuts, cold cereals	Brown thrasher; catbird; blue jay; chickadee; purple finch; sparrows; junco; tufted titmouse; cardinal; downy woodpecker; Carolina wren.

HOW TO MAKE A SUET HOLDER

To get started feeding birds in the yard, it is a good idea to begin in October with a few simple feeders. Keep them well stocked, and as they become used regularly, substitute more elaborate, permanent feeders.

As a starter, you should have two feeders to hold suet and two to hold seeds, or one combination feeder that will hold both suet and seeds.

SUET HOLDERS

Soap dish suet holder   *Suet holder made of planed lumber*   *Log suet holder*

The simplest kind of a suet holder is a wire soap dish that you can buy for twenty-five cents or so in any ten-cent or hardware store. This is the soap dish that resembles a small wire basket, and is about an inch deep, 4 inches wide, and 6 or 7 inches long. On each end are springs that are stretched around the faucets in the kitchen sink. To use it as a suet holder, get a piece of wood about 12 inches long, 5 inches wide, and an inch thick. About ½-inch from each end of the board, and in the center of the board, screw in a small hook—the kind that is used to hang cups in the kitchen closet (hardware dealers call them "cup hooks"). Stretch the springs of the soap dish around these hooks so that the open top of the soap dish is flat against the board.

Fasten the board securely to a tree or clothesline pole about head height above the ground. Place suet in the dish.

Another easy-to-make suet holder is simply a piece of natural wood (the bottom 18 inches of an old Christmas tree or other log) or an 18-inch-long piece 2 x 2 inches. Use a 1-inch or ¾-inch wood bit and drill three or four holes in each side of the wood, about an inch deep.

Stuff suet in these holes. Fasten a screw eye in the end, and hang the wood from a branch or on a clothesline pole.

If you use a piece of 2 x 2 that is planed smooth, use a saw to make some grooves around the piece of wood so that the birds have a place to cling as they feed.

HOW TO MAKE A SEED TRAY

The simplest kind of seed tray is a piece of board about 2 feet long, 10 inches wide, and an inch thick. Get some lath or similar wood 2

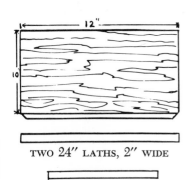

TWO 24" LATHS, 2" WIDE

TWO 10" LATHS, 2" WIDE

The parts of the seed tray, showing dimensions

SEED TRAY

The assembled seed tray

BRACES TO HOLD TRAY

The seed tray in place on a window sill outside of the house

inches wide by ½-inch thick and nail it around the edge of the board so that the seed will not blow off.

Fasten this board to your outside window sill, or to a pole or tree in the yard. Sprinkle seed of various kinds on the board.

Many hardware stores, garden supply shops, and florists sell bird seed. If you watch advertisements in the garden page of the Sunday paper, you will frequently find suppliers who sell bird seed. As a last resort, use "chicken feed" that can be purchased in most super markets in the suburbs or in feed stores in the country areas.

GENERAL RULES FOR BIRD FEEDING

In any case, here are a few general rules to follow in feeding birds:

Once you start feeding birds, keep it up all winter. Once birds become accustomed to feeding in your yard, they will rely on you for winter food.

Place your feeders near, but not in, shrubs, trees, or other places where birds can hide. Many birds are too wary to venture far from cover. They will not fly too far into the open to feed. Those that do, need cover to fly to in case a cat or hawk happens by and tries to catch them.

Try a variety of food until you find a combination that attracts the largest number of birds. You will soon find that certain foods are preferred by certain birds and that you can almost select the birds that you want by putting out the right kind of food.

Here's one way to find out what birds like most in the way of food:

Get a board about 2 feet long, 10 inches wide, and an inch thick. Drill some 1-inch holes through the board. Get some of the small paper cups that restaurants use to serve jelly for toast. Place the cups in the holes and nail the board to the window sill or to a tree or post.

Put a different kind of food (see chart on pp. 61-62) in each cup. Check the board every few hours to see which food birds eat first, which cup is emptied next, etc. In that way you can tell which food birds prefer, and which kinds to put out to attract certain birds.

Gull:

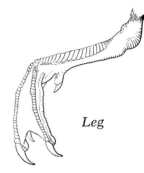

Bill

Leg

California gull in flight

HOW TO BUILD A TROLLEY FEEDER

You may find that at first birds are too wary to feed on your window sill and that they seem to prefer the feeders that are away from the house.

To attract them closer to the house, build a feeder, as is shown in the illustration below, that will hang on a wire or clothesline. Stretch a piece of wire or clothesline from a tree or post to the house window. Start with the feeder at the post or tree, some 50 feet from the house. Fill the feeder with the kind of food that birds seem to prefer.

When birds use the trolley feeder regularly and show no fear of it, move it a few feet closer to the house. Wait a few days until birds are accustomed to it again, then move it a few feet closer again.

Keep up this process every few days until the birds are feeding near the house. Then put food only on the window sill, or continue to feed them in the trolley feeder if the feeder is where you can watch it easily.

HOW TO FEED BIRDS IN THE HOUSE

If your mother doesn't object, and she probably won't, here's a stunt that will enable you to attract birds within the house. Blue jays, and even cowbirds or sparrows, will do it quite readily.

TROLLEY FEEDER

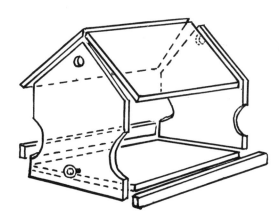

How the parts of the trolley feeder are assembled

The finished trolley feeder in use

Start with peanuts for jays or seeds for sparrows or cowbirds, and attract birds to your window sill. After the birds come regularly and feed without fear, open the window a little. When they get used to that, open the window still farther. Finally, get them accustomed to feeding on the window sill with the window wide open. It may take several days, with an hour or two a day getting them used to the open window. Next, move the feed from the feeder to the inside window sill, and give the birds time to become used to feeding on the sill just inside the window.

Then place a card table or other easily moved table, inside, up against the window sill, and put the food on the table near the window. When the birds become accustomed to feeding in the house on the table, move the food across the table to the other side. In a few days you can move the table back into the room a few feet. Finally, birds will fly to the window, perch on the sill, look into the room, fly in after food, and fly out the window again.

If you sit very quietly, not moving a muscle, they will even fly in while you are there and feed right before your eyes, almost from your own dining-room table. It's an interesting trick and a lot of fun.

Bald Eagle:

Head

HOW TO FEED BIRDS FROM YOUR HAND

Even more fun is feeding birds right from your hand. Here's how to do it:

Start by attracting birds to your window sill, and wait until they are accustomed to feed there. Then get a piece of wood about 1 inch by 2 inches and 2 or 3 feet long. Also get an old pair of gloves or a pair of inexpensive cotton work gloves.

Put one glove on the end of the wood and fasten it with a thumbtack. Slide the sleeve of an old coat or sweater on the wood so the sleeve comes right to the glove.

Push this "arm"—sleeve and glove—out the window and put the window down so it holds the "arm" in place, sticking out over the window feeder. Sprinkle some food on the glove. Leave it there for a week or so until the birds are used to it and eat the seed from the glove.

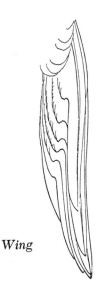

Wing

Foot

Tail

Then substitute your own arm for the wood. Put on the coat or sweater and the glove and poke your arm out the window.

Rest your arm on the window sill so it won't get tired and fill the palm of the glove with seed.

Very soon the birds will start eating right from your hand. The next step is to remove the glove and let the birds feed from your bare hand. That's really fun.

One bird watcher did it a little differently. He built a scarecrow out in his yard, using old clothes and an old hat to cover a wooden frame. The arms were outstretched. He put feed on the hat and in the hands, on the shoulders, and even in a corncob pipe in the scarecrow's mouth. After a few weeks birds were feeding all over the scarecrow—sitting on the hat, the shoulders, and the arms, and even feeding out of the corncob pipe.

Then one night the bird watcher took the scarecrow indoors and took off the clothes. The next morning at dawn he took the place of the scarecrow, wearing exactly the same clothes. Sure enough, the birds came quite readily and perched all over him as they fed on the food he had provided.

PERMANENT FEEDERS

The feeders described earlier are excellent for getting started and for discovering whether or not birds will feed in your yard and whether or not you are interested enough to keep up bird feeding as a hobby.

If you find that birds come regularly to your yard and that you want to stay at it for several years, it's time to make some permanent feeders—the kind that will last for a long time.

The kinds shown in the illustrations are good for this purpose. The weather vane feeder is an excellent one, for example. It turns with the wind so that birds are protected from the wind as they feed. More than that, strong wind will not blow the feed away.

The feeders with the glass top and back are fine for the window sill or a pole near the house. The food and birds are protected from wind or snow, and you can look through the glass and see what is going

Warbler:

Head

Beak

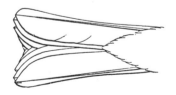

Tail

Leg

Wing

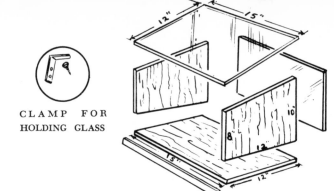

wooden feeder

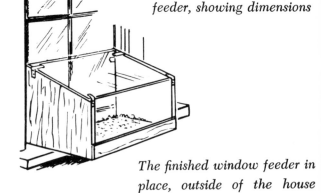

CLAMP FOR
HOLDING GLASS

PERMANENT FEEDERS

*The parts of a window
feeder, showing dimensions*

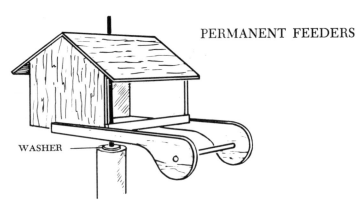

WASHER

Weather vane feeder that turns with the wind

*The finished window feeder in
place, outside of the house*

on inside. These are easy to make but require a little more care and
skill. They are more attractive to look at, too. If you want to try bird
photography, they are better for pictures.

HOW TO KEEP SQUIRRELS AND CATS AWAY

Many bird watchers who start back yard feeding discover that squirrels
find the feeders very quickly and eat up all the food before the birds
can get it. They also will scare away birds. Cats sometimes will
visit feeders and lie in wait for birds, trying to catch them as they
come looking for food. Cats may even climb poles or trees and scare
birds away.

   The answer, in part, is to put smooth metal around the pole or tree
so that the cat or squirrel cannot climb up. Use old tin cans or piece
of sheet metal and tack it around the tree or pole in a band about

COCONUT SHELL FEEDER

15 or 20 inches high, so that the animals cannot get a grip with their claws and climb over it. Place the band high enough so that the animals cannot jump over the metal and get a grip on the wood above it.

Another stunt is to place feeders on top of poles made from old pieces of pipe.

Squirrels frequently can jump to feeders that hang from trees, or from a tree to the pole on which the feeder is located. To make this impossible, get a piece of sheet metal and cut it in the shape of a big circle—2 feet in diameter. Cut a slot from one edge to the center of the circle. Then bend the metal until it forms a flat cone and fasten it with rivets or screws and nuts. Run the wire that holds the feeder through the center of the cone, so the cone forms a roof over the feeder. It will help to keep squirrels away.

GROUND-FEEDING BIRDS

Some birds prefer to feed on the ground, and although they will feed at feeders, they will be attracted more quickly if you feed them on the ground, where they are accustomed to feed naturally. Some of the sparrows, juncos, cowbirds, and doves are in this class.

Old Christmas trees make fine ground feeders. Chop off the branches from one side and save them. Drive a stake in the ground so that it sticks up about two feet above the ground. Nail the bottom of the tree to the top of the post so that the small end of the tree is on the ground and side from which you cut branches is down.

Use the branches you cut off to cover any open places in the tree. Sprinkle food in front and under the tree. The tree will provide protection from wind and snow. But if there are cats around, don't make this kind of feeder. It's too easy for the cats to catch the birds.

One of the best ways to get acquainted with birds is to attract them to your yard where you can watch them easily and learn all their markings and other characteristics that help identify them. Depending upon where you live, there are many different birds that will visit your yard. For real fun in winter, try feeding wild birds.

Chapter Seven

BACK YARD SANCTUARIES

In addition to birdhouses and feeders, there are two other methods of attracting birds to a back yard or park, both of which are as good or better all year round than either birdhouses or feeders. The first is bird baths and the second is plants of various kinds that attract birds.

BIRD BATHS

Many birds, like you or me, need water. They need it for drinking or for bathing. Bird baths are easy to make or buy and are a very effective way of attracting birds to the yard. Birds will be attracted to water at all seasons of the year.

Probably the easiest way to make a bird bath is to start with a top of a garbage can or trash can. The top will act as the bath, since it will hold water.

There are three ways of setting up the bath out in the yard. The easiest way is merely to lay it on the ground, pack some dirt around it to keep it steady, and fill it with water. But neighbors' dogs may drink the water or cats may try to catch the birds that go there for a drink.

A better way is to get a four-foot long piece of 4 x 4-inch wood or 2 x 4-inch and drive it into the ground so it stands up perfectly straight. Remove the handle from the can top and throw it away. Fasten the can top to the top of the post with three large screws. Before pushing or hammering the screws through the can, place a rubber or leather washer on the screw. When you screw the screw in tight, the washer will prevent the water from leaking out. Another way is to paint the inside of the can top with two or three coats of good white enamel. Usually the enamel will seal the holes.

Another good way to mount the can top is to use a piece of clay sewer pipe (available at plumbing supply shops or lumber yards) about eight inches in diameter. Set one end of the pipe a few inches in the ground so that it will not tip over.

Then find a rock or brick that will slide down inside the pipe. Fasten a piece of wire around the brick and fasten the other end of the wire to the handle of the can top. The distance between the brick and top should be about 12 inches.

Place the can top on the pipe so that the brick hangs down on the inside of the pipe. The brick will keep that can top from blowing or falling off when birds perch on it.

Paint the pole or pipe dark green or white so that it blends in with the garden background. Also, be sure to place the bath near some shrubs so that birds can fly to cover if a cat or hawk comes by. When birds are soaking wet, they have a difficult time flying too far, too fast.

It's also a good idea to place a large stone or rock in the middle of the bath for birds to perch on before they jump in for a bath, or to stand on while they drink.

Sometimes it takes birds quite a while to find the bird bath and you feel that they will never find it. Here's a way to help them find it:

Use an old coffee can or other tin can, and hang it 2 or 3 feet over the bird bath. Using a small nail, punch a hole in the can just above the bottom rim. Whittle a small wooden plug and insert it in the hole from the inside.

Fill the can with water. Adjust the plug so that the water drips out very slowly, a few drops a minute, into the bath. That drip, both the sound and the ripples on the bath, will attract birds.

WINTER BIRD BATHS

Birds need water in winter, too, but frequently the cold weather will freeze the bath so birds cannot drink the water.

You can make a freeze-proof bath quite easily by using two old coffee cans, an electrical extension cord and socket, and a 10- to 40-watt bulb, depending upon how cold it is.

Cut a small hole in one can. Push one end of the cord through the hole and fasten the socket to it. Place the bulb in the socket.

On the other end of the wire, fasten a plug. Place the can on the outside window sill, or on the back porch railing if you have a porch light. Connect the plug to an electrical outlet in the house, or on the porch, so that the bulb lights up.

Place a second can on top of the first and fasten it with wide tape. Run the tape around both cans where they meet.

Put water in the top can. The heat from the bulb will keep the water from freezing except in very cold weather, and birds will have water to drink all day long.

PROVIDING NATURAL FOOD AND COVER

While birdhouses and feeders will attract birds at certain times of year, and bird baths will attract them any time, probably nothing is more attractive than the right kinds of plants.

Birds are wild animals. By instinct they feed on wild fruits, seeds, and insects, and nest in natural places such as trees, shrubs, or open fields. They will eat food you put out and will nest in man-made houses but they prefer natural food and nesting sites to man-made substitutes. The people who have been most successful in attracting birds to back yard sanctuaries have done so by planting the right kind of food shrubs and shrubs that provide cover and shelter.

It does not require too much space devoted to shrubs to attract

FOR WATER

The two parts of the bird bath

WINTER BIRD BATH

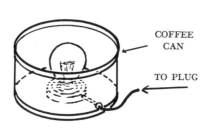

COFFEE CAN

TO PLUG

The bottom part of the bird bath, showing socket, bulb, and extension cord

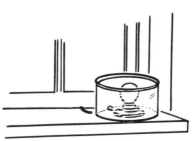

The bottom part of the bird bath, in place on window sill outside of house

TAPE

The finished bird bath filled with water, showing the two halves fastened together with tape

some birds. But generally it is necessary that the shrubs be planted in masses—that is, covering a solid area from the ground up to seven or eight feet high, or higher. Here a shrub and there a shrub is better than nothing. But it is not as good as planting several shrubs in relatively small areas, or even a row of shrubs or trees that birds can use as a "roadway" across the yard.

In thinking of shrubs that are attractive to birds, think of them as being in two groups: those that provide hiding places and shelter from enemies; and those that provide food. Fortunately many shrubs that are most attractive to look at are also good for birds.

Whippoorwill:

Head

FOOD SHRUBS

Dogwood may grow as a shrub or a small tree, depending upon the kind it is. But any dogwood is one of the best food plants for birds you can find. It has attractive blossoms in the spring, and even in winter some kinds have reddish, greenish, or yellowish stems and twigs that are colorful. It will grow almost anywhere. More than ninety kinds of birds are known to eat the fruit (berries) on dogwood, among them being quail, flickers, bluebirds, catbirds, thrashers, robins and other thrushes, waxwings, grosbeaks, sparrows, and purple finches.

Beak

Elderberry is another shrub that is used for food by many different birds. It has a purplish black fruit that may be used for jams or jellies. Some birds will nest in elder thickets if the shrub is large enough to provide good cover. Among the birds that eat elderberry are: quail, woodpeckers, kingbirds, phoebes, mockingbirds, catbirds, thrashers, bluebirds, vireos, grosbeaks, towhees, thrushes, and sparrows.

Wildrose will make an attractive hedge or fence row in a yard. It grows as a low shrub or can be trained to grow on a trellis. When the blossoms are gone, you will see a red "hip," as the seed pod is called, and this is what birds eat. More than forty birds feed on wild roses, among them being: grouse, quail, pheasants, thrushes, robins, and cardinals.

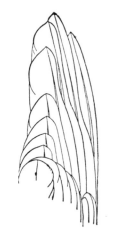

Wing

Blueberries which may be low-growing shrubs or quite high shrubs, depending upon location and kind, are easily grown in the yard

Tail

Foot

Young kingbirds

or garden. They are well known as fruit and are prized by such birds as: grouse, quail, bluebirds, chickadees, titmice, catbirds, thrashers, robins, thrushes, waxwings, orioles, grosbeaks, towhees, and king birds.

Blackberries and raspberries are also common fruits that we eat. They are easily grown in a garden or yard and are one of the best plants for birds. More than 150 kinds of birds are known to feed on these berries: thrushes, quail, sparrows, bluebirds, robins, grosbeaks, catbirds, woodpeckers, kingbirds, waxwings, vireos, orioles, cardinals, towhees, etc. The blossoms are known to attract hummingbirds.

Holly is an attractive shrub for any yard, since the leaves stay green all winter. At least forty kinds of birds will eat holly berries: grouse, quail, sapsuckers, mockingbirds, bluebirds, thrushes, waxwings, etc.

These are only a few of many plants that may be used in back yards, gardens, or other areas to attract birds. The fruit of many of them stays on all winter and will provide food at a time when birds need it most.

COVER SHRUBS

In the same way that most food shrubs can serve two purposes—beauty in the yard and perhaps food for you as well as for birds—other shrubs can be planted that provide nesting places for birds as well as added beauty in the yard.

Generally small trees or shrubs that do not lose their leaves in winter make excellent cover. That means trees or shrubs such as hemlock, cedar, or spruce.

Hemlock is used frequently as a hedge. It grows quite densely when the tops are cut back, and makes an attractive hedge for a fence line. It provides good cover and nesting sites for several birds, and even food for winter birds such as siskins or crossbills.

Cedar also makes a good fencerow or hedge and is easily grown. In addition to providing nesting sites for birds, it provides food for at least fifty birds, i.e., robins, waxwings, thrushes, bluebirds, grosbeaks.

Spruces, when planted rather close together along a fence line or in clumps, are good for birds. Several back yard birds will nest in them, including robins, jays, doves, and grackles. The seeds in the cones provide winter food for crossbills, siskins, and chickadees.

Yew is an attractive, generally low-growing evergreen shrub, and, when it grows densely, will provide good nesting sites for birds. Its red berries also provide food.

One of the best shrubs for nesting sites in the yard is a rambler rose. It is especially good if it grows in a large clump or bush rather than on a trellis or arbor. Song sparrows seem to like roses for nesting sites, and since they often raise two broods of young a year, a dense clump of rambler roses will provide "music" as well as flowers for most of the spring or summer.

Reddish egret feeding in surf

Marsh hawk

Killdeer on nest in gravel pit

Canyon wren

Parent feeding five- or six-day-old catbirds

Western gulls

Male Attwater's prairie chicken

HOW TO ATTRACT HUMMINGBIRDS

Hummingbirds will be attracted by many garden flowers or shrubs. Generally, however, they prefer blossoms that are reddish or orange in color.

Consequently, plants such as azaleas, columbine, phlox, delphinium, geranium, cardinal flower, scarlet runner bean, hollyhocks, beebalm, and morning-glories will attract these interesting tiny birds. It's well worth-while to plant some of these easy-to-grow flowers just for hummingbirds—if for no other reason.

A variety of plants usually is better than a large number of plants all the same kind. If you have a yard or other place where you can set out some of these food and cover shrubs, you can easily have your own "sanctuary"—a place where birds will come to feed or nest every year. A natural sanctuary such as this is better than an artificial one and is much easier to care for.

But even if you cannot plant shrubs, knowing that birds use the plants for food or shelter can be helpful to you. Look around in neighbors' yards, or in parks or public gardens, for these shrubs or trees. Then watch them regularly, and you will see more birds.

Chapter Eight

BIRD PHOTOGRAPHY

Bird photography is a sport that may easily provide all the thrills of big-game hunting or game fishing. The nice thing about it is that you can go camera hunting right in your back yard or in neighboring parks, woods, fields, or marshes. Traveling long distances is not necessary. More than that, you can hunt at any time of year. There are no closed seasons and you do not need expensive licenses.

If you are successful, you will have a trophy that is every bit as spectacular as a tiger skin or a moose head. For a good photograph of a bird in flight, or poised on a branch, or feeding along the waters' edge may be a work of art. To get it takes more skill, more time, more patience, and more ability than it takes to shoot an animal or a flying duck.

To be a successful bird photographer, first you must know something about birds. Then you need some basic equipment.

Close-up lens

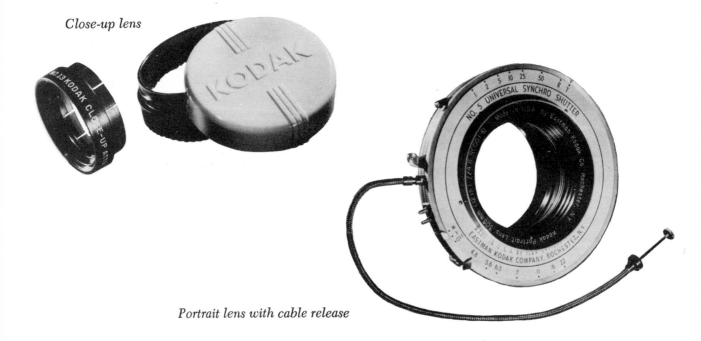

Portrait lens with cable release

Pelican colony

LEARNING BIRD HABITS

After you have watched birds at a feeder or bird bath, or feeding naturally on the ground or along the water's edge, you will notice that they have certain habits that will help you photograph them.

For example, if you have built a bird bath such as the one described in the last chapter and have placed a stone or rock in the middle, you will probably notice that a bird perches on the rock for a second or two before it takes a bath.

If you watch birds at a feeder, you probably have noticed that birds perch in a spot on the feeder before starting to feed. Perhaps they perch on the tree trunk, or atop the post, or on top of the feeder. But usually they will sit there for a second or two, or even for a minute before they sample the seed or suet that you have put out for them.

In any case, they sit still for a short period of time, looking around to be sure the coast is clear. That's the time to photograph them. That's what is meant by "know your birds." Watch them long enough to observe the habits that will make your photography job easier.

CAMERA EQUIPMENT

Fortunately, for bird photography, you do not need expensive equipment. You can use almost any kind of camera and get bird pictures. But like any other kind of photography, the better equipment you have, the better pictures are possible, provided you know how to use your equipment.

However, two things are important for bird photography, and without them you are wasting time and film trying to get pictures. You will need a camera to which you can attach a portrait attachment or telephoto lens; and you will need something to set off the camera from some distance away. If it has a flash attachment too, so much the better. You can make a device for setting off the camera from a distance; but you must buy a portrait attachment, supplementary lens, or telephoto.

The portrait attachment or telephoto is important because you need some way of magnifying the bird or enlarging it on the negative. Birds are quite small, and at six to fifteen feet, which is about the closest you can get to them, the image on the negative may be so small that you can barely see it. If you try to enlarge the picture with an enlarger, you have to "blow it up" so much that the grain of the film will greatly detract from the picture.

A portrait attachment is a lens that fits over the regular lens on the camera. Read the instructions that come with the attachment so you will know how to focus. Portrait attachments generally cost only a couple of dollars or less.

Telephoto lenses magnify a great deal, and are used to replace the regular lens in certain cameras. They are quite expensive, but they are better for bird photography.

REMOTE CONTROL OR BLINDS

The secret of good bird photography is to get as close to the bird as possible without scaring it away. You can do this in two ways: Either use a blind as is described on page 45 or place your camera close to the bird while you stand fifty or a hundred feet away. This system is called "remote control."

To use a blind, set it up eight to fifteen feet from where the bird will be. Set your camera on a tripod inside the blind. Focus the camera on the spot where the bird will be and wait for it to come.

Titmouse:

Beak

Wing

Leg

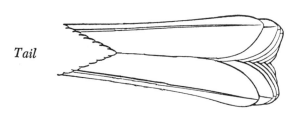

Tail

An easy-to-make remote-control gadget can be made from a hinge, rubber bands, a metal cable release, a small nail or stick, and a long piece of string. The illustration shows how to do it.

Fasten the hinge on the tripod so that it opens and closes easily. Place the cable release through a screw hole in the hinge so that the closing hinge will press the release and open the shutter. Fasten two or three strong rubber bands around the hinge so as to hold it closed.

Force the hinge open and hold it open with a small nail or a stick of wood. Tie a long piece of strong string to the nail or stick. When you pull the cord and pull the nail or stick out, the hinge closes and automatically opens the shutter by pressing the cable release.

SHUTTER SPEED

If you have a choice of shutter speed on your camera, use at least one-hundredth of a second. If not, wait for the bird to be absolutely still before taking the picture. Birds are small, but they move quickly and can easily cause a blur on the negative. Wait till they quiet down and pose just right. You will "miss" many pictures at best without trying for long shots that rarely turn out well.

FOCUS

If you can adjust the lens opening on your camera, close it down as far as possible, depending upon the shutter speed. There's a good

REMOTE CONTROL PICTURE TAKER

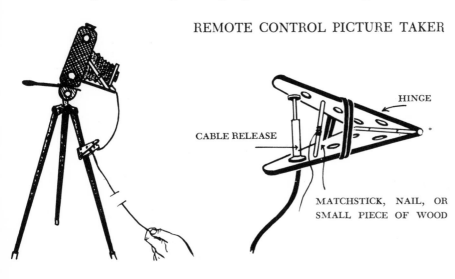

CABLE RELEASE

HINGE

MATCHSTICK, NAIL, OR
SMALL PIECE OF WOOD

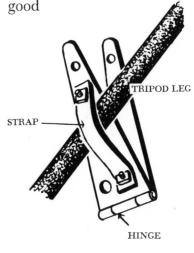

TRIPOD LEG

STRAP

HINGE

A remote control gadget in use   *The assembled remote control gadget*   *How the remote control gadget is attached to the tripod leg*

reason for this. The smaller the lens opening, the greater the depth of focus will be. When you photograph as close as eight feet, the depth of focus is small enough at best. All the extra you can get is to the good.

It is important to focus carefully and accurately. An out-of-focus bird is a queer-looking animal and does not make a good picture. But when you take pictures of birds as close as you must to get good pictures, sometimes the front half of the bird will be in focus and the back half will not be. That's why careful focusing and depth of focus are important. You want good, sharp pictures with the entire bird in sharp detail.

If it is a tossup as to whether you shoot at a hundredth or a fiftieth at let's say f. 6.3 or f. 8, use the fiftieth at f. 8 and wait till the bird is still. If you can shoot at a hundredth of a second at f. 8, so much the better. If smaller openings are possible, use them at one-hundredth of a second.

FILMS

For black-and-white film, panchromatic films with a Weston rating of 50 are probably best for all-around work. But you will need good light. If you can use flash bulbs, use films of this sort. If you cannot use a flash and the light is poor, use one of the "super" panchromatic films with a Weston rating of 100. Be sure to have all your films fine-grain developed.

Woodcock on nest

Red-winged blackbird

If you use color in the woods or where the light is not good, you almost have to use a flash for best results. With a flash you must have a color filter; these cost under $5.00, price varying with the size of your lens. Color film is slow, and frequently requires lens openings greater than you can get on the average camera. A good rule to follow is to expose the film twice as long as you would expose a black-and-white film—for example, one-fiftieth of a second with a color film when one-hundreth would work with black-and-white.

TRIPODS

Always use a tripod when taking bird pictures, except of birds in flight. First, it's easier. You can set the camera on a tripod, focus the camera on the perch, and wait for the bird to come along. Second, you can be more sure of sharp pictures. Bird photography is difficult as it is without having to worry about holding the camera steady. Tripods will help eliminate this problem.

BACKGROUNDS

"Watch your background" is an old adage in photography. How many times have you seen snapshots of friends, showing a person with a clothesline seeming to go in one ear and out the other, or a picture of a person with a tree growing out of his head? How many pictures have you seen where the background was so confusing that the main subject was lost?

Bandtailed pigeon squab

Young bald eagle

Half-grown horned owl

With bird photography, backgrounds are especially important. The bird may blend into the leaves so you cannot see it, or the background of leaves may be confusing so that your attention is attracted to it instead of to the bird. Try to get the bird against a plain background—sky or water or distant landscape. If you focus critically on the bird, the background may be way out of focus and thus be unobjectionable. Another stunt is to try to get the bird in good light so that the background is underexposed and quite dark. The contrast will make the bird stand out.

But there are other tricks to try, too. They are rather easy. One of them can be used near a bird bath.

Two or three feet from your bird bath, drive a stake in the ground so that the top is a foot or two higher than the bath. Drill a hole in the stake on the side toward the bath, about a foot higher than the bath. Cut a branch of a tree or shrub and insert it in the hole so the branch extends out over the bath.

Most birds will perch on the branch for a few seconds before taking a drink. When you find exactly where they perch, focus on that spot and wait for the bird to come. If you arrange the pole right and place the camera correctly, you should be able to get the bird in bright sunlight and standing out against the sky or other uncluttered background.

The second stunt is much the same, but makes use of food to attract birds.

Drive two stakes in the ground about 3 feet apart, one 3 feet high and one 5 feet high. Place a wooden tray of food on the short stake and insert a branch in a hole in the long stake so that it is a foot or two above the food. As birds come to feed, they will perch on the branch for a minute or two before jumping down to feed.

The same sort of trick also works sometimes at birdhouses.

Bald eagle

NATURAL SETTINGS

Many times as you go on bird watching hikes you will find places where birds feed or bathe in natural areas. There may be a small pool or a spring in the woods where they come to drink, or an old stump or log near where they feed.

Watch the spring for a while or find a favorite perch. Try putting some food on the stump or log, and perhaps you can attract birds that you do not see in your yard.

Use the same techniques as you do in your yard—either a blind or a remote-control gadget.

In winter you will frequently find ducks in parks or nearby ponds. You can attract them to camera range by feeding them corn or bread crusts.

They may become tame or they may come to feed only after you have walked away. The trick is to put "bait" (food) in the water, set up your camera on a tripod, hook up your remote-control gadget, and then walk away and hide behind a tree. When they come to feed, *click*, you have another picture.

Sandpipers along the beach can be photographed in much the same way. Push two little sticks in the sand or place two shells a few feet apart. Focus on the space between the sticks or shells, with the camera on a tripod ten feet away. Hook up the remote control and walk back a hundred feet. Wait for the birds to walk in between the shells. Or ask a friend to walk slowly along the beach and "walk" the birds between the shells. When they get in just the right position, take the picture.

Bird photography is a lot of fun. It's not easy, but with practice it is not difficult. You can get pictures that will be the best kind of decoration for your room or den. But most important, you will have a picture record of your hobby and the birds you see. Try bird photography for some real thrills and adventure.

Mourning dove

Chapter Nine

WHERE TO FIND BIRDS

Scattered around the United States are many public and private bird sanctuaries and refuges. The best way to find out about them is to ask an experienced bird watcher who lives in your area. If you do not know a bird watcher, ask your local state conservation agent or game protector. He will be able to tell you about the best places to go. Many state road maps list and show the locations of game refuges and public areas where you may find unusual birds.

In addition, there are excellent aviaries to be found in many zoos, which house numbers of different bird species. At the end of this chapter you will find a list of zoos in the United States and Canada, which house live birds.

NATIONAL PARKS AND MONUMENTS

National parks and historical parks are, in effect, bird sanctuaries or refuges. They are areas where all plant and animal life is protected for the enjoyment of all visitors. These areas are set aside to protect some unusual scenic or historic area, but in the process they frequently become excellent places to look for birds.

Following is a list of national parks; if unusual or distinctive birds are to be found in any of these places, the list includes this information. For further information, write to National Park Service, Washington, D. C., for pamphlets on each park. Many of these separate pamphlets describe the animal life to be seen in the park.

Thrush:

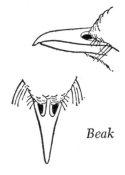

Beak

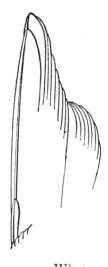

Wing

Tail

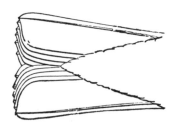

Leg

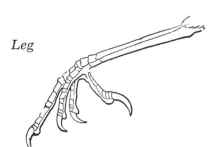

Refuge sign on highway

NATIONAL PARKS

ACADIA NATIONAL PARK   Mount Desert Island, off the coast of Maine.
   Distinctive birds: Osprey, bald eagle, ruffed grouse, cormorant,
   common loon, herring gull, and great blue heron are among the
   larger birds found in the park; while thrushes, warblers, and other
   songbirds are present during the summer.

BIG BEND NATIONAL PARK   On the border in West Texas.
   Distinctive birds: Road runner, Mearn's and scaled quail, Inca dove,
   and cactus wren are common birds. The couch jay, colima warbler,

Texas blue-throated hummingbird, Mexican phainopepla, and dwarf red-shafted flicker found to the southward, here reach their northern limits. Other birds common to the park are pointed redstart, Stephens' vireo, and lucifer hummingbird.

BRYCE NATIONAL PARK Southern Utah.
Bird life is abundant during the summer months.

CARLSBAD CAVERNS NATIONAL PARK Near the southeastern corner of New Mexico.
Distinctive birds: Scaled quail, canyon wren, cactus wren, western mockingbird, Pyrrhuloxia, and many kinds of hawks and owls are frequently seen.

CRATER LAKE NATIONAL PARK Located on the summit of the forested Cascade Range in southern Oregon.
Distinctive birds: Golden and bald eagle, falcon, osprey, horned owl, California gull, cormorant and Sierra grouse, red-breasted nuthatch, Sierra brown creeper, Sierra junco, mountain chickadee, western evening grosbeak, western tanager, spotted and green-tailed towhee, and Townsend's solitaire.

EVERGLADES NATIONAL PARK Southern tip of the Florida Peninsula.
Distinctive birds: Roseate spoonbill, wood and white ibis, seven species of heron—the Ward's, great white, little blue, green, black-crowned night, yellow-crowned night, and Louisiana—the American egret, the snowy and reddish egret, the water turkey or anhinga, chuck-will's-widow, swallow-tailed kite, short-tailed hawk, white-crowned pigeon, purple and Florida gallinules, bald eagle, and turkey.

GLACIER NATIONAL PARK In the Rockies of northwestern Montana.
Distinctive birds: Common loon, red-breasted, hooded, and American mergansers, osprey, bald and golden eagles, ruffed Richardson and Franklin grouse, white-tailed ptarmigan, red-shafted flicker, Rocky Mountain jay, Clark crow, northern varied thrush, Alaska three-toed woodpecker, pine siskin, rufous hummingbird,

Sparrow:

Beak

Wing

Tail
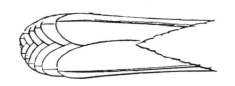

Foot-structure

Cormorant colony

water ouzel, mountain bluebird, and crossbill.

GRAND CANYON NATIONAL PARK On Arizona's Coconino Plateau.
Distinctive birds: Golden and southern bald eagles, white-faced glossy ibis, Gambel's quail, avocet, northern and Wilson's phalaropes, road runner, Nuttail's poorwill, Pacific nighthawk, black-chinned, broad-tailed, and calliope hummingbirds, long-crested, Woodhouse, and pinyon jays, canyon wren, sage thrasher, chestnut-

backed and mountain bluebirds, Scott's and Bullock's orioles, lazuli bunting, and Mexican crossbill.

GRAND TETON NATIONAL PARK Northwestern Wyoming.
Distinctive birds: Barrow's golden-eyed duck, American merganser, Richardson's and gray ruffed grouse, western horned owl, red-naped and Natalie's sapsucker, Clark crow, long-tailed and mountain chickadees, water ouzel, mountain bluebird, Bohemian waxwing, and lazuli bunting.

GREAT SMOKY MOUNTAINS NATIONAL PARK In western North Carolina and eastern Tennessee.

HAWAII NATIONAL PARK Located partly on the Island of Hawaii and partly on the Island of Maui.
Distinctive birds: Akiapolaau; a brown-and-white thrush known as the amoo; a member of the flycatcher family called the elepaio; the amakihi; the apapane of red, black, and white plumage; and iiwi.

ISLE ROYALE NATIONAL PARK Wilderness island in northern Lake Superior belonging to Michigan.
Distinctive birds: Osprey, Canada jay, herring gull, downy and pileated woodpeckers, chickadee, American merganser, black duck, and bald eagle.

LASSEN VOLCANIC NATIONAL PARK Northern California.

MAMMOTH CAVE NATIONAL PARK Southwestern Kentucky.
Distinctive birds: Eastern bobwhite, spotted sandpiper, yellow-billed and black-billed cuckoos, screech and northern barred owls, chuck-will's-widow, eastern whippoorwill, northern flicker, and the large, spectacular pileated woodpecker.

MESA VERDE NATIONAL PARK Southwestern Colorado.

MOUNT MCKINLEY NATIONAL PARK Central Alaska.
Distinctive birds: Willow ptarmigan, the rare surfbird, yellow-billed loon, whistling swan, lesser snow goose, western harlequin and old-squaw ducks, golden and bald eagles, little brown crane, Pacific

golden plover, wandering tattler, long-tailed jaeger, Arctic tern, snowy owl, Alaska three-toed woodpecker, and Bohemian waxwing.

MOUNT RAINIER NATIONAL PARK   Cascade Mountains, Washington. *Distinctive birds:* Sooty grouse, white-tailed ptarmigan, band-tailed pigeon, golden and bald eagles, saw-whet and pigmy owls, Alaska three-toed and the Lewis woodpeckers, Voux swift, rufous hummingbird, Steller's jay, northern raven, Clark crow, white-winged and sitke crossbill, Hepburn rosy finch, western tanager, northern violet-green swallow, and water ouzel.

Phalarope

Downy young hooded merganser

OLYMPIC NATIONAL PARK Located in Northern Colorado's snow-capped Rocky Mountains.

Distinctive birds: Gadwall, green-winged and blue-winged teals, ring-neck and redheaded duck, Wilson's phalarope, Howell's nighthawk, northern white-throated swift, broad-tailed hummingbird, Rocky Mountain and long-crested jays, water ouzel, ptarmigan, rosy finch, chestnut-backed and mountain bluebirds, yellow-headed blackbird, and western tanager.

SEQUOIA AND KINGS CANYON NATIONAL PARK Adjoin each other on the west slope of the Sierra Nevada of California.

Distinctive birds: Golden eagle, red-tailed and sparrow hawks, Sierra grouse, mountain quail, band-tailed pigeon, several species of hummingbirds, eleven kinds of woodpeckers, blue-fronted and long-tailed jays, Clark's nutcracker, and water ouzel.

SHENANDOAH NATIONAL PARK Blue Ridge Mountains.

Distinctive birds: Ruffed grouse, bobwhite, northern raven, crow, white-breasted nuthatch, Carolina chickadee, tufted titmouse, car-

Redheaded duck

dinal, various woodpeckers and owls, rose-breasted grosbeak, scarlet tanager, blue-headed and red-eyed vireos, numerous warblers, Carolina junco, thrasher, catbird, robin, and ruby-throated hummingbird.

WIND CAVE NATIONAL PARK   Black Hills of South Dakota.
Distinctive birds: Prairie sharp-tailed grouse, red-shafted flicker, mourning dove, redheaded woodpecker, Say's phoebe, and horned lark.

Sierra grouse

Adult eastern green heron

YELLOWSTONE NATIONAL PARK   Northwestern Wyoming.
  Distinctive birds: White pelican, white trumpeter swan, eagles,
wild geese and ducks, osprey and gulls.

YOSEMITE NATIONAL PARK   Sierra Nevada in California.
  Distinctive birds: Steller's jay, water ouzel.

ZION NATIONAL PARK   Southern Utah.
  Distinctive birds: Over 150 varieties of birds have been recorded in
the area, including the water ouzel, which inhabits the cool canyons.

Heron:

NATIONAL MONUMENTS

The following national monuments are also excellent places to look for birds.

Head

Name of Monument   *Location*

ARCHES *Southeastern Utah*

BADLANDS *In Southern South Dakota's White River Badlands*

BLACK CANYON OF THE GUNNISON *Western Colorado*

CAPITOL REEF *South central Utah*

CAPULIN MOUNTAIN *Northern New Mexico*

CEDAR BREAKS *Southern Utah*

CHANNEL ISLANDS *Consist of Santa Barbara and Anecapa Islands off the coast of southern California*

CHIRICAHUA *Southern Arizona*

COLORADO *West central Colorado*

Leg

CRATERS OF THE MOON *Southern Idaho*

DEATH VALLEY *Eastern California*

DEVIL POSTPILE *Eastern California*

DEVILS TOWER *Northeast corner of Wyoming*

DINOSAUR *Northeastern Utah and northwestern Colorado*

FOSSIL CYCAD *Southwest corner of South Dakota*

GLACIER BAY *On the coast of southern Alaska*

Close-up of young cormorants

Name of Monument	Location

JACKSON HOLE *Adjoins the eastern and northern boundaries of Grand Teton National Primeval Park in northwestern Wyoming.*

GRAND CANYON *Northern Arizona*

GREAT SAND DUNES *South central Colorado*

JEWEL CAVE *Southwestern South Dakota*

JOSHUA TREE *Southern California*

KATMAI *Southeast corner of the Alaska Peninsula*

LAVA BEDS *Northern California*

LEHMAN CAVES *Eastern Nevada*

MUIR WOODS *Located near the California coast, ten miles north of the Golden Gate Bridge*

NATURAL BRIDGES *Southeastern Utah*

OREGON CAVES *In the Siskiyou Mountains of southwestern Oregon*

ORGAN PIP CACTUS *Southwestern Arizona*

PETRIFIED FOREST *Eastern Arizona*

Fledgling desert horned owl

PINNACLES *West central California*

RAINBOW BRIDGE *Southeastern Utah*

SAGURARO *Southern Arizona*

Close-up of avocet wading

Name of Monument   *Location*

SHOSHONE CAVERN   *Located among the scenic cliffs of Cedar Mountain, four miles southwest of Cody in northern Wyoming.*

SUNSET CRATER   *North central Arizona*

TIMPANOGOS CAVE   *Northern Utah*

WHEELER   *La Garita Mountains of southern California*

WHITE SANDS   *Southern New Mexico*

ZION   *Southwestern Utah*

WILDLIFE REFUGES

For a list of wildlife refuges administered by the U. S. Fish and Wildlife Service, write to: Division of Information, Fish and Wildlife Service, Washington 25, D. C. Many of these refuges are excellent places to go to look for birds at certain times of year.

STATE REFUGES

For lists of state-operated refuges, write to the individual and agency in following list for the desired state:

State	Official Title of Director	Agency	Location
ALABAMA	Chief, Div. of Game Fish, and Seafoods	Dept. of Conserv.	Montgomery
ARIZONA	Director	Game & Fish Dept.	Phoenix
ARKANSAS	Secretary	Game & Fish Comm.	Little Rock
CALIFORNIA	Executive Officer	Div. of Fish & Game	Sacramento
COLORADO	Executive Director	Game & Fish Dept.	Denver
CONNECTICUT	Superintendent	Bd. of Fisheries and Game	Hartford
DELAWARE	Chief Game Warden	Board of Game & Fish Commissrs.	Dover
FLORIDA	Director	Game & Freshwater Fish Comm.	Tallahassee
GEORGIA	Director	Fish & Game Dept.	Atlanta
IDAHO	Director	Fish & Game Comm.	Boise
ILLINOIS	Director	Fish & Game Comm.	Springfield
INDIANA	Director	Fish & Game Div.	Indianapolis
IOWA	Chief of Fish & Game	Conserv. Comm.	Des Moines
KANSAS	Director	Forestry, Fish & Game Comm.	Pratt
KENTUCKY	Director	Div. of Game & Fish	Frankfort
LOUISIANA	Commissioner	Dept. of Wildlife & Fisheries	New Orleans
MAINE	Commissioner	Inland Fisheries & Game Dept.	Augusta
MARYLAND	Director	Dept. of Game and Fish	Baltimore
MASSACHUSETTS	Dir., Div. of Fisheries & Game	Dept. of Conserv.	Boston
MICHIGAN	Chief, Game Div.	Conserv. Dept.	Lansing
MINNESOTA	Dir. of Game & Fish	Dept. of Conserv.	St. Paul
MISSISSIPPI	Director	State Fish and Game Comm.	Jackson

WHERE TO FIND BIRDS

99

Wren:

Beak

Wing

Leg

Tail

State	Official Title of Director	Agency	Location
MISSOURI	Director	Dept. of Conserv.	Jefferson City
MONTANA	State Fish & Game Warden	Dept. of Fish & Game	Helena
NEBRASKA	Chief Conserv. Off.	Game, Forestation and Parks Comm.	Lincoln
NEVADA	Director	Fish & Game Comm.	Reno
NEW HAMPSHIRE	Director	Fish & Game Dept.	Concord
NEW JERSEY	Secy., Div. of Fish & Game	Dept. of Conserv. and Econ. Dev.	Trenton
NEW MEXICO	Director	Game & Fish Dept.	Santa Fe
NEW YORK	Dir., Div. of Fish and Game	Conserv. Dept.	Albany
NORTH CAROLINA	Director	Wildlife Resources Comm.	Raleigh
	Commissr. Marine Fisheries	Dept. of Conserv. and Dev.	Raleigh

MY HOBBY IS
BIRD WATCHING

100

Pair of quail—male at left, female at right

Young great horned owls in nest

State	Official Title of Director	Agency	Location
NORTH DAKOTA	Commissioner	Game & Fish Dept.	Bismarck
OHIO	Chief Wildlife Div.	Dept. of Nat. Resources	Columbus
OKLAHOMA	Director	Fish & Game Dept.	Oklahoma City
OREGON	State Game Dir.	State Game Comm.	Portland
PENNSYLVANIA	Exec. Director	Game Comm.	Harrisburg
RHODE ISLAND	Administrator	Div. of Fish and Game, Dept. of Agric. & Conserv.	Providence
SOUTH CAROLINA	Chief Game Warden	Off. of Chief Game Warden	Columbia
SOUTH DAKOTA	Director	Game, Fish & Parks Dept.	Pierre
TENNESSEE	Dir., Div. of Game and Fish	Dept. of Conserv.	Nashville
TEXAS	Exec. Secy.	Game, Fish and Oyster Comm.	Austin

State	Official Title of Director	Agency	Location
UTAH	Director	Fish & Game Dept.	Salt Lake City
VERMONT	Dir. of Fish and Game Serv.	Fish & Game Comm.	Montpelier
VIRGINIA	Exec. Secy.	Comm. of Game and Inland Fisheries	Richmond
WASHINGTON	Chairman	State Game Comm.	Olympia
WEST VIRGINIA	Director	Conserv. Comm.	Charleston
WISCONSIN	Supt. of Fish Management	Conserv. Comm.	Madison
WYOMING	Game & Fish Commissr.	St. Game & Fish Dept.	Cheyenne

ZOOLOGICAL GARDENS

Here is a list of chief zoos in the United States and Canada which house a collection of birds:

ALBUQUERQUE, N. M. Rio Grande Zoo, City Hall. Hours: 8:00 A.M. to 8:00 P.M. daily. Free.

ATLANTA, GA. G. V. Cress Zoo, 601 City Hall. Hours: 8:30 A.M. to 5:30 P.M. daily. Free.

AVALON, CALIF. Catalina Bird Park, c/o Santa Catalina Island Co., Box B-2. Hours: 7:00 A.M. to 4:00 P.M. (winter); 7:00 A.M. to 7:00 P.M. (summer). Free.

BALTIMORE, MD. Baltimore Zoo, Druid Hill Park. Hours: 10:00 A.M. to 5:00 P.M. daily. Free.

BROOKFIELD, ILL. The Chicago Zoological Park. Hours: 10:00 A.M. to 6:00 P.M. (summer); 10:00 A.M. to 5:00 P.M. (spring and fall); 10:00 A.M. to 4:30 P.M. (winter) weekdays, an hour later on Sundays. Children free; adults, $.25 Monday, Tuesday, Wednesday and Friday—free the rest of the week and on legal holidays.

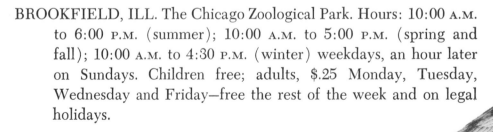

Crow

BUFFALO, N. Y. Buffalo Zoological Gardens. Hours: 8:00 A.M. to 7:00 P.M. daily. Free.

CALGARY, ALBERTA, CANADA. Calgary Zoological Gardens and Natural History Park, St. George's Island. Hours: 8:00 A.M. to 7:00 P.M. daily. Free.

CANTON, OHIO. Canton Zoo, Nimisilla Park. Hours: 10:30 A.M. to 4:30 P.M. daily. Free.

Swallow:

Beak

CATSKILL, N. Y. Catskill Game Farm, Inc. Open April 15 to Dec. 1. Hours: 9:00 A.M. to 6:00 P.M. daily. Adults, $.85; children, $.30.

CHICAGO, ILL. Lincoln Park Zoological Gardens, Lincoln Park. Hours: 9:00 A.M. to 5:00 P.M. (winter); 10:00 A.M. to 6:00 P.M. (summer). Free.

CINCINNATI, OHIO. Zoological Society of Cincinnati, 3400 Vine St. Hours: 9:00 A.M. to 7:00 P.M. (summer); 9:00 A.M. to 6:00 P.M. (spring and fall); 9:00 A.M. to 5:00 P.M. (winter) daily. Children (2 to 15), $.15; over 15 and adults, $.50.

CLEVELAND, OHIO. Cleveland Zoological Park, Brookside Park. Hours: 9:00 A.M. to 8:00 P.M. (summer); 9:00 A.M. to 5:00 P.M. (winter) daily. Free.

COLUMBUS, OHIO. Columbus Zoological Gardens, Rt. 1, Powell, Ohio. Hours: 9:30 A.M. to sunset daily. Children (under 12) free; over 12 and adults, $.25.

DALLAS, TEX. Dallas Zoo, Marsalis Park, 524 S. Marsalis Ave. Open until dark daily. Free.

DENVER, COLO. Denver Zoological Gardens, City Park. Open from daylight to dark daily. Free.

DETROIT, MICH. Detroit Zoological Park, 8450 W. Ten Mile Road, Royal Oak. Open second Thursday in May through first Sunday in November. Hours: 10:00 A.M. to 5:00 P.M. weekdays, 9:00 A.M. to 6:00 P.M. Sundays and holidays. Free.

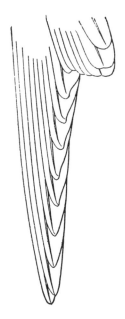

Wing

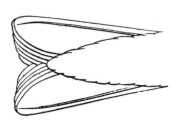

Tail

Leg

Heavy concentration of ducks

DULUTH, MINN. Duluth Zoo, 208 City Hall. Hours: 10:00 A.M. to dark daily. Free.

EDMONTON, ALBERTA, CANADA. Borden Park Zoo, City of Edmonton Parks Dept., Civic Block. Hours: 8:00 A.M. to 10:00 P.M. daily. Free.

EVANSVILLE, IND. Mesker Park Zoo. Hours: 9:00 A.M. to 5:00 P.M. daily. Free.

Rump of canvasback *Foot of mallard*

Typical Ducks:

FORT WORTH, TEX. Fort Worth Zoo, Forest Park. Hours: 6:00 A.M. to 7:00 P.M. daily. Free.

FRESNO, CALIF. Roeding Park Zoo, 894 W. Belmont Ave. Hours: 8:00 A.M. to 5:00 P.M. daily. Free.

GRAND RAPIDS, MICH. The John Ball Park Zoo, 201 Market St. S.W. Hours: 8:00 A.M. to 4:30 P.M. (winter); 9:00 A.M. to 8:00 P.M. (summer). Free.

HOUSTON, TEX. Houston Zoological Garden, 509 City Hall. Hours: 9:00 A.M. to 6:00 P.M. daily. Free.

JACKSONVILLE, FLA. Jacksonville Municipal Zoo, Star Route, Heckscher Drive. Hours: 8:00 A.M. to 6:00 P.M. daily. Free.

KANSAS CITY, MO. Swope Park Zoological Gardens, 6701 Lister. Hours: 10:00 A.M. to 6:00 P.M. daily. Free.

KENDALL, FLA. Miami Rare Bird Farm, Inc., Box 100. Hours: 9:00 A.M. to 6:00 P.M. daily. Adults, $1.00; children, $.35.

LANSING, MICH. Potter Park Zoo, 202 City Hall. Hours: 8:00 A.M. to 5:00 P.M. daily. Free.

LINCOLN, NEBR. Lincoln Municipal Zoo. Hours: 9:00 A.M. to 4:45 P.M. Free.

LITTLE ROCK, ARK. Little Rock Municipal Zoo, Room 211, City Hall. Hours: 9:30 A.M. to 4.30 P.M. (summer); 9:00 A.M. to 6:00 P.M. (winter)—buildings close 4:30 P.M. daily. Free.

LOS ANGELES, CALIF. Griffith Park Zoo, Box 284. Hours: 8:30 A.M. to 4:30 P.M. Free.

MADISON, WISC. Henry Vilas Park Zoo, 1317 Wingra Drive. Hours: 8:30 A.M. to 5:00 P.M. daily. Free.

MANITOWOC, WISC. City of Manitowoc Zoo. Hours: Sunrise to sundown. Daily. Free.

Foot of buffle-head

Rump of ruddy duck

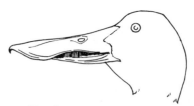

Head of shoveller

MEMPHIS, TENN. Overton Park Zoo, Overton Park. Hours: 9:30 A.M. to 5:30 P.M. weekdays, 9:30 A.M. to 6:00 P.M. Saturday and Sunday. Free.

MIAMI, FLA. Crandon Park Zoo, 4000 Crandon Blvd., Biscayne Key. Hours: 9:00 A.M. to 6:00 P.M. daily. Free.

MILWAUKEE, WISC. Washington Park Zoological Gardens, 4500 W. Vliet St. Hours: 9:30 A.M. to 4:50 P.M. daily. Free.

MINOT, N. D. Minot Park District, Box 548. Hours: 8:00 A.M. to 10:00 P.M. (summer); 8:00 A.M. to 5:00 P.M. (winter). Free.

MOOSE JAW, SASKATCHEWAN, CAN. Moose Jaw Wild Animal Park Society, Can. Zool. Society. Hours: 10:00 A.M. to 9:00 P.M. daily. Cost—$.50 per car.

NEW ORLEANS, LA. Audubon Park Commission. Hours: 9:00 A.M. to 6:00 P.M. Free.

NEW YORK, N. Y. Central Park Zoo, 64th St. and 5th Ave. Hours: 11:00 A.M. to 5:00 P.M. daily. Free.

New York Zoological Park, 185th St. & Southern Blvd. Hours: 10:00 A.M. to 4:30 P.M. or 6:30 P.M. (depending on season, holidays, etc.). Free except Tuesday, Wednesday, Thursday, when charge is adults, $.10; children (5 to 11), $.05; holidays free.

Staten Island Zoo, 614 Broadway, Staten Island 10. Hours: 10:00 A.M. to 5:00 P.M. (10:00 A.M. to 6:00 P.M. on summer Sundays and holidays). Free.

NORRISTOWN, PA. Elmwood Park Zoo, City Hall, DeKalb and Airy Sts. Hours: 10:00 A.M. to 6:00 P.M. daily. Free.

Western bluebird at its nest hole in a dead willow

OAKLAND, CALIF. Knowland State Park and Arboretum, 98th Ave. and Mountain Blvd. Hours: 8:00 A.M. to 6:00 P.M. daily. Facility fee, $.25.

OKLAHOMA CITY, OKLA. Lincoln Park Zoo, 404 Municipal Bldg. Hours: 7:00 A.M. to sundown daily. Free.

PHILADELPHIA, PA. Zoological Society of Philadelphia, 34th St. and Girard Ave. Hours: April 1 to October 1—10:00 A.M. to 5:00 P.M. Monday to Friday, 10:00 A.M. to 6:00 P.M. Saturday, 10:00 A.M. to 7:00 P.M. Sundays and holidays; October 1 to April 1—10:00 A.M. to 5:00 P.M. daily. Adults, $.50; children (5 to 11), $.25.

PITTSBURGH, PA. Highland Park Zoological Gardens. Hours: 9:00 A.M. to 5:00 P.M. (winter); 9:00 A.M. to 6:00 P.M. weekdays, 9:00 A.M. to 7:00 P.M. Sundays and holidays (summer). Free.

POCATELLO, IDAHO. Ross Park Zoo.

PORTLAND, ORE. Washington Park Zoo, 115 City Hall. Hours: 10:00 A.M. to dark daily. Free.

PRAIRIE DU CHIEN, WISC. Rose Park Zoo. Hours: 7:00 A.M. to 7:00 P.M. daily. Open six months. Adults, $.50; children, $.25.

QUEBEC, CANADA. Quebec Zoological Garden, Orsainville (via Charlesbourg), R.R. 54. Hours: 9:00 A.M. to 8:00 P.M. daily (open six months). Adults, $.25.

RACINE, WISC. Racine Zoological Park, 2131 N. Main St. Hours: 10:00 A.M. to 5:00 P.M. (winter); 10:00 A.M. to sundown (summer) daily. Free.

RAPID CITY, S. D. Hill City Zoo, Box 1701. Hours: 8:00 A.M. to 5:00 P.M. daily. Adults, $1.00; children (5 to 12), $.50.

ROCHESTER, N. Y. Seneca Park Zoo. Hours: 10:00 A.M. to 7:30 P.M. Daily. Free.

SACRAMENTO, CALIF. William Land Park Zoo, Room 305, City Hall. Hours: 8:00 A.M. to 4:30 P.M. daily. Free.

ST. LOUIS, MO. St. Louis Zoological Garden, Forest Park. Hours: 9:30 A.M. to 5:00 P.M. (March 1 to November 30), 9:30 A.M. to 4:30 P.M. (December 1 to February 28). Free.

ST. PAUL, MINN. Como Park Zoo, 1224 N. Lexington St. Hours: 10:00 A.M. to 4:30 P.M. weekdays; 10:00 A.M. to 6:30 P.M. Sundays. Free.

SALT LAKE CITY, UTAH. Hogle Zoological Garden, P. O. Box 2337. Open 10:00 A.M., closing time fluctuates with seasons. Free.

Tracy Aviary, Liberty Park. Hours: 10:00 A.M. to 6:00 P.M. Open everyday but Monday. Free.

SAN ANTONIO, TEX. San Antonio Zoo, 3919 N. St. Marys. Hours: 8:00 A.M. to 5:00 P.M. (winter); 8:00 A.M. to 6:30 P.M. (summer). Adults, $.25; children, $.10.

SAN DIEGO, CALIF. Zoological Gardens of San Diego, Box 551. Hours: 8:00 A.M. to 5:00 P.M. daily. Adults, $.40; children free.

SAN FRANCISCO, CALIF. San Francisco Zoological Gardens. Hours: 10:00 A.M. to dark daily. Free.

SEATTLE, WASH. Woodland Park Zoological Garden. 5400 Phinney Ave. Hours: 8:00 A.M. to dusk daily. Free.

SHEBOYGAN, WISC. Volrath Park Zoo, 1320 Niagara Ave. Hours: 8:00 A.M. to 7:00 P.M. (summer); 10:00 A.M. to 5:00 P.M. (winter). Free.

SILVER SPRINGS, FLA. Ross Allen's Reptile Institute. Hours: 8:00 A.M. to 8:00 P.M. daily, May-Sept.; 8:30 A.M. to 7:00 P.M., Oct.-April. Adults, $1.15; children and servicemen, $.60.

STROUDSBURG, PA. Pocono Wild Animal Farm, R. D. 1. Hours: 8:00 A.M. to 6:00 P.M. Open May to November. Adults, $.60; children, $.25.

Two white pelicans and a cormorant in flight

THOUSAND OAKS, CALIF. World Jungle Compound, Box 151. Hours: 10:00 A.M. to 5:00 P.M. daily. Adults, $.50; children, $.25. Free admission to Los Angeles and county schools in classes.

TOLEDO, OHIO. Toledo Zoological Gardens. Hours: 10:00 A.M. to 7:00 P.M. (summer); 10:00 A.M. to 5:00 P.M. (winter). Winter, free; summer, $.20 weekdays, $.25 Sundays and holidays.

WASHINGTON, D. C. National Zoological Park, Adams Mill Road nr. Ontario Place. Hours: 9:00 A.M. to 4:30 P.M. daily (winter); 9:00 A.M. to 5:00 P.M. sundays and holidays (winter); 9:00 A.M. to 5:00 P.M. daily (summer); 9:00 A.M. to 5:30 P.M. Sundays and holidays (summer). Free.

WHEELING, W. VA. Wheeling Park, National Road. Hours: 7:30 A.M. until dark daily. Free.

Chapter Ten

PUBLICATIONS ABOUT BIRDS

BOOKS

Both of the following books are helpful to the beginner and experienced bird watcher alike. Each contains lists of places to look for birds and directions for finding them. Use the book suited to the area in which you live or the area where you expect to look for birds.

WHERE TO FIND BIRDS

A Guide to Bird Finding East of the Mississippi, by Olin S. Pettingill. New York, Oxford University Press, $6.50.

A Guide to Bird Finding West of the Mississippi, by Olin S. Pettingill. New York, Oxford University Press, $6.00.

BACK YARD BIRDING

All of the following books describe various ways of attracting birds to the back yard or garden.

Audubon Guide to Attracting Birds, by John H. Baker. New York, Doubleday, Doran and Company. $2.50. (Out of print.)

Birds in the Garden and How to Attract Them, by Margaret McKenny. New York, Reynal & Hitchcock, $3.95.

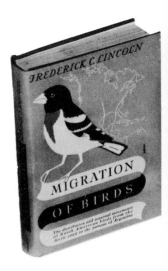

"Migration of Birds"

Birds in Your Back Yard, by Ted S. Pettit. New York, Harper & Brothers, $3.00.

Songbirds in Your Garden, by John K. Terres. New York, Thomas Y. Crowell Company, $3.95.

GENERAL BOOKS ON BIRDS

The following books are recommended additions to the bird hobbyist's library:

Birds of the Ocean, by W. B. Alexander. New York, G. P. Putnam's Sons, $7.50.

Birds of the World, by Paul Barruel. New York, Oxford University Press, Inc., $12.50.

Birds over America, by Roger Tory Peterson. New York, Dodd, Mead & Company, $6.00.

Land Birds of America, by Robert Cushman Murphy and Dean Amadon. New York, McGraw-Hill Book Company, $5.95.

Migration of American Birds, by Frederick Lincoln. New York, Doubleday & Company, $1.50.

Natural History of the Birds of Eastern and Central North America, by E. H. Forbush and John May. Boston, Houghton Mifflin Company, $7.50.

BIRD PHOTOGRAPHY

Nature Photography Round the Year by Percy Morris. New

"Birds in Your Backyard"

York, Appleton-Century-Crofts, $4.00. Best all-around book on nature photography, including birds.

Stalking Birds with Color Camera—published by the National Geographic Society, 16th & M Streets, N. W., Washington, D. C., $7.50. Many natural color photographs of birds in action.

REGIONAL OR STATE BOOKS

Every birder will get a great deal of help from books or other publications on birds relating to his specific region or state. The following list is not too complete, since many regional publications were published years ago. They are now out of print, and have not been included in this list. Therefore, if you do not find a publication listed here for your area, there may be a copy of an out-of-print regional publication available for reference at your library. Some of the more recent books and pamphlets are listed here with the suggestion that those bird watchers who do not find one listed for their area can look at one from a neighboring region.

Birds of Alabama, by Arthur H. Howell. Department of Game and Fisheries, Montgomery, Ala., 1928.

Birds of Arkansas, by W. J. Baerg. University of Arkansas Experiment Station, Fayetteville, Ark., 1931, $1.50. Write to: The University of Arkansas Bookstore, Fayetteville, Arkansas.

Florida Bird Life, by Alexander Sprunt, Jr. National Audubon Society, 13 Fifth Avenue, New York 28, N. Y., $12.50.

Birds in Kansas, by Arthur L. Goodrich. Kansas State Board of Agriculture, Topeka, Kans., 1945. Free.

Birds of New Mexico, by Florence Merriam Bailey. New Mexico Department of Game and Fish, Sante Fe, N. M., 1928. $15.00.

Birds of Buckeye Lake, Ohio, by Milton B. Trautman. University of Michigan, Ann Arbor, Mich., 1940. $4.50.

Wyoming Bird Life, by Otto McCreary. University of Wyoming, Laramie, Wyo., 1937. $2.00. Write to Burgess Publishing Company, Minneapolis, Minn.

Birds of the Pacific Coast, by W. A. Eliot. New York, G. P. Putnam's Sons, $5.50.

Birds of the Pacific States, by Ralph Hoffmann. 1927. Houghton Mifflin Company, Boston, Mass., $5.00.

Introduction to Western Birds, Lane Publishing Company, Menlo Park, California, $1.50.

Natural History of the Birds of Eastern and Central North America, by E. H. Forbush, revised and abridged by John B. May. Houghton Mifflin Company, Boston, Mass., 1939, $7.50.

California and ring-billed gulls and Caspian terns

Avocet:

BIRD MAGAZINES

Here is a list of recommended bird and nature magazines which have articles of current interest for the birder:

Head

Audubon Field Notes—published bimonthly by the National Audubon Society. It is devoted to results of bird watching. Yearly subscription—$3.00.

Audubon Junior News—official publication of Audubon Junior Clubs. Published five times a year by National Audubon Society. Yearly subscription—$1.25. About 16 pages; book reviews, nature in general, but greatest emphasis on birds. Club news from all the states. Illustrations plentiful. Nature crossword and other puzzles, quiz, etc. Ages—about 10 to 15.

Audubon Magazine—published bimonthly by the National Audubon Society. Yearly subscription—$3.00. 1130 Fifth Avenue, New York 28, N. Y.

Junior Natural History—published monthly by the Museum of Natural History, Central Park West at 79th Street, New York 24, N. Y. Yearly subscription—$1.50. About 22 pages; at least one article on birds; many illustrations for children; book reviews. Pen-pals exchange on nature, birds, etc. Ages—10 to 15.

Nature Magazine—published ten times a year by the American Nature Association, Washington, D.C. Frequent articles on birds, although the content covers all phases of nature. Yearly subscription —$4.00.

Bill

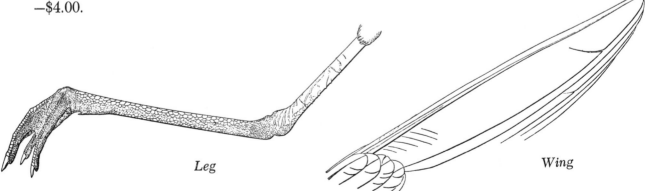

Leg

Wing

BIRD MAGAZINES FOR THE EXPERIENCED BIRD WATCHER

The Auk—published quarterly. To get it you must be a member of the American Ornitholigist's Union. Free to members. Membership is $4.00 per year. Send money to Treasurer: Charles G. Sibley, Fernow Hall, Cornell University, Ithaca, N. Y.

The Condor—Cooper Ornithological Society, Museum of Vertebrate Zoology, Berkeley, Calif. A bimonthly publication. Yearly subscription—$5.00.

The Wilson Bulletin—a quarterly publication. Yearly subscription —$3.00. Write to: Leonard C. Brecher, Treasurer, *The Wilson Bulletin,* 1900 Spring Drive, Louisville 5, Ky.

Snowy egret feeding on tadpoles in desert waterhole

AUDUBON PUBLICATIONS

To obtain the following reprints, send name, address, and money to the National Audubon Society, 1130 Fifth Avenue, New York 28, N. Y. If six or more copies are ordered, add five cents postage.

FIVE CENT MAGAZINE REPRINTS

The Case Against Trapping California Condors
Concerning Predators
An Ornithologist Looks at Conservation

MY HOBBY IS
BIRD WATCHING

116

TEN CENT MAGAZINE REPRINTS

Care and Feeding of Wild Birds
A Closer Look at the Killers (Predation)
Flower Gardens for Birds
How to Take a Breeding Bird Census
Know your Binoculars
Let's Get Ready for Winter Feeding
Lost—Part of a Continent (The Whooping Crane)
More Birds for Your Garden
Out of the Grey Mist (Stormy Petrel)
Persecution or Freedom? (Bald Eagle)
A Price on His Golden Head (Golden Eagle)
A Sanctuary on the Perkiomen (Mill Grove)
Snobber, Sparrow De Luxe
Vanishing Wings Over the Sawgrass (Everglade Kite)
Wings Across the Moon (Night Migration)
Winter Problems at the Feeding Station

"Songbirds in your Garden"

LEAFLETS AND PAMPHLETS

Leaflets are 5¼ x 8½ inches. A separate color picture and an outline drawing for coloring of the bird is inserted in each leaflet.

To obtain the following leaflets, send name, address, and money to the National Audubon Society, 1130 Fifth Avenue, New York 28, N. Y. Single copy is $.10 postpaid. If six or more 5-cent leaflets are ordered, add five cents for postage.

Auklet, Crested
Avocet
Bittern, American
Blackbird, Red-winged
Blackbird,
    Yellow-headed
Bluebird
Bobolink
Bob-white
Bunting, Indigo
Bunting, Lazuli
Bunting, Snow
Bush-tit
Cardinal
Catbird
Chickadee
Cormorant,
    Double-crested
Creeper, Brown
Crow
Cuckoo, Yellow-billed
Dove, Mourning
Duck, Canvas-back
Duck, Mallard
Duck, Pintail
Eagle, Bald
Egret, Snowy
Finch, House
Finch, Purple
Flicker
Flicker, Red-shafted
Flycatcher, Crested

Goldfinch
Goose, Canada
Goose, Emperor
Grackle
Grosbeak, Black-headed
Grosbeak, Rose-breasted
Gull, Herring
Hawk, Red-shouldered
Hawk, Red-tailed
Hawk, Sharp-shinned
Hawk, Sparrow
Heron, Great Blue
Hummingbird, Anna's
Hummingbird,
    Ruby-throated
Hummingbird,
    Three Western
Jay, Blue
Jay, Steller's
Junco, Slate-colored
Killdeer
Kingbird
Kingfisher
Kinglets, The
Lark, Horned
Longspur, Alaska
Loon
Martin, Purple
Meadow Lark
Mockingbird
Nighthawks
Nuthatches

Oriole, Baltimore
Oriole, Orchard
Ovenbird
Owl, Barn
Owl, Burrowing
Owl, Screech
Phoebe
Pigeon, Passenger
Quail, California
Redstart
Robin ·
Sandpiper, Spotted
Sapsucker,
    Yellow-bellied
Sparrow, Chipping
Sparrow, English
Sparrow, Song
Sparrow, Tree
Sparrow,
    White-throated
Starling
Stilt, Black-necked
Swallow, Barn
Swift, Chimney
Tanager, Scarlet
Thrasher, Brown
Thrush, Wood
Titmouse, Tufted
Towhee, Red-eyed
Turkey Vulture
Veery
Vireo, Red-eyed

"Nature Magazine"

Warbler, Audubon's
Warbler, Chestnut-sided
Warbler, Yellow
Waxwing, Cedar
Whippoorwill
Whooping Crane
Woodpeckers, Downy
and Hairy

Woodpecker,
Redheaded
Wren, Carolina
Wren, House
Yellowthroat

Birds of Florida

Birds of the Lower
Rio Grande

Birds of Southern
California

Birds of Central
California

When ordering the following illustrated pamphlets from the National Audubon Society, add five cents for postage.

Bird Day, $.10
Bird Migration, $.10
Birdhouses and Feeding Stations, $.15
Building a Nature Interest, $.10
Electric Nature Games, $.10
Field Activities, $.10
Forests, $.10
Grassland, $.10
How Should Nature Be Taught?, $.10

Nature Photography, $.10
Nature Trails, $.10
Owl Study, $.10
Small Nature Museums, $.10
Soil—How Wildlife Depend Upon It,
    $.10
Swamps and Marshes, $.10
Water—Life-blood of the Earth, $.10
Winter Feeding, $.10

GOVERNMENT PAMPHLETS

If you wish to obtain any of the following government pamphlets, write to: Superintendent of Documents, Government Printing Office, Washington, D. C.

Attracting Birds, by W. L. McAtee. Conservation Bulletin No. 1, Fish and Wildlife Service, $.10. Covers feeders and bird baths and a little on planting to attract birds.

Fruits Attractive to Birds, Northwestern States. Leaflet BS-41, free.

Fruits Attractive to Birds, Rocky Mountain States. Leaflet BS-42, free.

Fruits Attractive to Birds, Northern Plains States. Leaflet BS-43, free.

Fruits Attractive to Birds, Northeastern States. Leaflet BS-44, free.

Fruits Attractive to Birds, California. Leaflet BS-45, free.

Fruits Attractive to Birds, Great Basin States. Leaflet BS-46, free.

Fruits Attractive to Birds, Southwestern States. Leaflet BS-47, free.

Fruits Attractive to Birds, Florida. Leaflet BS-50, free.

Migration of Birds. Catalog No. I 49.4: 16, 35¢

All of the following may be obtained from Department of Agriculture:

Homes for Birds by W. L. McAtee and E. R. Kalmach. Conservation Bulletin No. 14, 15¢.

How to Attract Birds in Northeastern States. Farmers' Bulletin 621, $.05.

How to Attract Birds in Northwestern States. Farmers' Bulletin 760, $.05.

How to Attract Birds in Middle Atlantic States. Farmers' Bulletin 844, $.05.

How to Attract Birds in East Central States. Farmers' Bulletin 912, $.05.

NOTE: Many pamphlets go out of print and new ones come in. The best thing is to write to: Fish and Wildlife Service, U. S. Department of the Interior, Washington, D. C., requesting list of publications. This list covers all current books, pamphlets, leaflets, etc., and prices.

Golden eagle with prey

Chapter Eleven

ITEMS OF INTEREST TO

BIRD HOBBYISTS

HOW TO BECOME A JUNIOR BIRD CLUB MEMBER

If you are a boy scout, girl scout, a camp fire girl, or just a young person interested in the fascinating bird world, one of the best ways of getting to know more about it is to join an Audubon Junior Club.

Perhaps there is a junior club in your community. You can find out about it by writing directly to the Audubon Junior Clubs, 1130 Fifth Avenue, New York 28, New York.

But, even if your neighborhood does not have such a club, it is easy to form a new one. All you have to do is to get at least nine other young people besides yourself, and an adult, usually a teacher, youth leader, or parent to sponsor your club.

Each club member pays dues of 15¢ a year. A new club pays a registration fee of $1.00. The adult club leader should send the registration fee and the dues by check or money order to the Audubon Junior Clubs in New York.

Each child receives an Audubon Junior Club membership button and a 16-page Nature Notebook containing color pictures of birds, nature stories, and space for your own nature notes and calendar.

A 100-page Nature Program Guide is sent to the Club Leader, which helps him organize nature projects, games, and other activities. Each club also receives a year's subscription to Audubon Junior News, the best children's magazine about birds. Club members write many of the articles and draw many of the illustrations appearing in Audubon Junior News.

Audubon Jr. Clubs chart ▶

AUDUBON MATERIALS

The following items may be obtained from the National Audubon Society, 1130 Fifth Avenue, New York 28, N. Y. Send name, address, price of item, and additional for postage if indicated.

BIRD CARDS

Colored bird portraits (post card size) from original paintings by Allan Brooks and Roger Tory Peterson. Descriptive text on reverse side. Packed fifty in a box—$1.50.

Eastern
    Summer—$1.50. Winter—$1.50. Spring—$1.50.

Western
    One set—$1.50 (add ten cents postage).

From Wild Bird Series originated by Betty Carnes
Executed in Water Color by Francis Lee Jaques

Audubon Society post cards

CHARTS

Set of four charts in full color by Jacob Bates Abbott. Summer Birds, Winter Birds, Birds of Prey, Game Birds. Size 20 x 30 inches. Ready for hanging. Sold only in sets of four—$3.00.

Set of four charts in full color by Jacob Bates Abbott. Summer Birds (continued), owl and two mammal charts—size 20 x 30 inches. Ready for hanging. Sold only in sets of four—$3.00 (add twenty cents postage).

POST CARDS

Picture post cards showing birds in color can be obtained from the National Audubon Society, 1130 Fifth Avenue, New York 28, New York.

Eastern Set A—10 in a set....$.30
Eastern Set B—10 in a set.... .30
Western—10 in a set .... .30

SLIDES AND FILMS

The Photo and Film Department of the National Audubon Society has slides and films for sale and rental. A complete listing of the Audio-Visual materials is contained in their catalog, which costs twenty cents a copy.

BIRD FILE

This is a specially designed, systematic file for keeping all your bird notes in one place. Space is provided for migration, nesting, rarities, etc. This file will prove helpful for both beginners and experts alike. It provides a nucleus of 250 5″ x 7″ cards for Northeastern U. S. birds.

   This file costs $3.00 (add twenty cents postage).

Close-up of glossy ibis

ALPHABETICAL INDEX

126

127

American and snowy egrets in nesting colony